MAKE W[ ] CHASE YOU

How To Fill Your Life With Hot Women
- The Complete Course -

Justin Rigney

Disclaimer

Contents

Chapter 6: Attraction Phase 3 - Fascination

Foreword: It's All About You

Gentlemen,

It's time to start attracting the women you want into your life. It's time to start making them chase *you*. It's time to become the guy you've always wanted to be; the guy who is magnetic and seems to attract women effortlessly.

You can become that guy. Yes, really. Even if you don't believe it at this very moment.

If you're willing to commit yourself to this course. If you're willing to take action to change yourself. Then you can become the kind of guy that women find irresistible -- no matter where you're starting from today.

It doesn't matter what your experience level is with women right now. It doesn't matter what your face looks like (yes, really). All that matters is that you're willing to change and willing to follow the steps in this course, even if they seem scary.

Commit yourself to that and in 25 days you will transform into the kind of guy that women feel an uncontrollable attraction toward. Women will start to compete with each other for your attention.

If that sounds like what you want for your life, then the first thing you must understand is that attracting women is all about *you*. Not them.

The world is full sexy women.

It will be full of sexy women no matter what you decide to do with this course. If you decide to read through this course and then do nothing, the world will still be full of sexy women.

They will just sleep with other guys. **Guys who made different choices than you.**

On the other hand, if you decide to dedicate yourself to this course. If you take the information, absorb it, and make it your own. If you transform yourself into the person that this course will show you how to become. If you practice improving yourself daily. If you force yourself to complete every Action Step. Then your life with women will change quickly, dramatically, and for the better.

Women will be chasing you. Women will be sleeping with you. Women will be pushing each other out of the way to get you.

This transformation will ultimately come down to a choice that you must make. This course will guide you in meticulous, step-by-step detail what needs to be done. But at the end of the day, <u>you must choose to do it</u>.

And let's be perfectly honest. The choices you will encounter in this course **are going to make you uncomfortable.** Because they will go against the most fundamental of human instincts.

What instinct is that? Well of course it's survival, right?

Wrong.

The most basic human instinct is to stay comfortable. Humans will do anything to avoid discomfort. Anything.

If survival was the most basic instinct, why would alcohol, cigarettes, drugs and fast food be so popular? We all know that stuff will kill you.

People aren't doing *anything they can to survive* when they consume alcohol, cigarettes, drugs and fast food.

So why are they consuming it?

Because it makes them comfortable. They are used to it. It's familiar.

They are knowingly sacrificing their survival for the sake of comfort. That's how powerful the instinct is to *stay comfortable*.

Right now, in this moment, you are a man who doesn't attract women. Or doesn't attract enough women. Or doesn't attract hot women. Or doesn't attract the right kind of women.

Why?

Only one reason. Because it's comfortable.

You want to attract more women. Hotter women. You tell yourself that all the time.

You genuinely believe it.

But despite everything you say, think, and believe, there's one thing getting in the way.

It's that getting where you want to be with women will require you to be uncomfortable, at least at the beginning.

So you don't do it. Your subconscious fights it to the bitter end. It does anything it can to avoid being uncomfortable. **People's subconscious would rather be miserable and comfortable, than happy and uncomfortable.**

If you don't believe that, just look at all the unhappy marriages in the world.

There is one underlying reason why miserable couples stay together.

Because it's familiar. Because it's comfortable.

So what's the difference between you and the guys you see getting all the hot women?

Is it that they were born comfortable? Is it that they found a magic way to just be comfortable?

No. They were uncomfortable too.

Did that register?

THEY WERE UNCOMFORTABLE TOO.

The only difference between them and you is that they were uncomfortable, and they did it anyway.

They made the choice. They made the decision that they would transform themselves into men who attract women effortlessly. No matter what it took. No matter how scary it was. No matter how uncomfortable it got.

Now it's your turn to make a choice. You have to choose to get uncomfortable.

Think about it for a day. Ponder it. It's not for everybody.

The idea of getting uncomfortable is now planted in your mind.

But you will need to keep reinforcing this idea as we go through the course. You will need to reinforce that getting uncomfortable is good. That it's what you want. That you're going to fight through the discomfort, whatever it takes.

Why?

Because as soon as you first start feeling uncomfortable, your subconscious will try every trick in the book to stop you. You may get upset. You may get scared. You may say: "that's not me" or "I can't do that." Your subconscious will fight furiously against the decisions you need to make.

That's when you need to reinforce the idea that getting uncomfortable is what you want. That you're willing to fight through 25 days of discomfort to arrive at a lifetime of pleasure with beautiful women. That you're going to do it anyway, no matter what.

No self-made success story got there without discomfort along the way. So grab a sticky note and write this down and post in on your bathroom mirror:

Being uncomfortable is what I want. On the other side of discomfort is a land filled with beautiful women.

Reinforce that message every morning and every night for the next 25 days. Just don't forget to tuck the note away inside the medicine cabinet when you start bringing hotties over to spend the night.

*****

Before we start the course, I'd also like to share with you my favorite story about Tony Robbins.

This story is not about what he teaches, but about the man himself.

We all know that Tony Robbins is arguably the greatest self-help guru of all time.

But why is he that?

How did he become that?

Was he born with special powers? Did he attend some secret school nobody else knew about? Did he drink the right Kool Aid?

Of course not. He was just a regular dude. Just like me and just like you.

I heard an interview with Tony where he was asked that very question. How did he become what he is today?

How did he go from being broke, overweight, and living in some crappy apartment, to the world-renown phenomenon that he became?

His answer was that he made a decision. A decision to change his circumstances, no matter what it took. No matter how scary it was. No matter how uncomfortable it got.

And a decision is a powerful thing. If you really commit to it and allow nothing to get in the way, a decision can transform your life.

Then Tony said my favorite line of all time. Referring to himself (referring to the Tony Robbins that he had become), he said this:

"I created that fucker out of nothing."

See. Just a normal dude who made a decision to change and refused to let anything get in the way.

That's exactly what you can accomplish using this course. You can create the man you've always wanted to be, out of nothing.

And here is a critical point:

Right now, you're not attracting women (or enough women, or enough hot women, whatever the case may be) because of a decision.

That's right. You are currently <u>making the choice to NOT attract these women</u>.

You've made this choice whether you know it or not. And whether you like it or not.

And everything in your life, from the way you look, to the way you act, to the way you carry yourself, to your demeanor, to your confidence, to everything, is a reflection of that choice.

It's essentially self-fulfilling. You've chosen that and now your life reflects that.

If you're ready, the time has now come to make a different choice.

No matter what.

I hope you're ready for a wild ride.

Chapter 1: Mental Overhaul

The World Will Accept What You Show It

Let's start with a reality check.

The world is indifferent to whether you attract women effortlessly or attract women not at all.

Let's look at the most important part of that statement: *the world is indifferent to whether you attract women effortlessly.* Said differently: the world is perfectly fine if you live a life filled with beautiful women.

There is no worldly force out there stopping you from attracting the 9s and the 10s. There is no fairness moderator saying the distribution of women must be equal among men.

The only thing moderating your success is yourself. You are showing the world that your success with women should be moderated (this is the decision you've made that we discussed earlier).

If you've read this far in the course, then you've now made a different decision: the decision to transform yourself. The first step is to transform what you believe.

Below is the belief system of the Carefree Man. A man who wholeheartedly show these beliefs to the world is irresistibly attractive to women.

When you first read these, it's likely you won't wholeheartedly believe them. That's because it's almost impossible to believe something that is drastically different than your personal experience.

However, the fact that you may not believe them today is perfectly fine. Just be open minded enough to let each belief be a seed planted in your subconscious. As we go through the course, those seeds will flourish.

Remember that life is short. And it can easily pass you by. In this life you can believe anything you want. The belief system you have today must not be fetching the results you want out of life, otherwise why would you be in this course?

So let those beliefs go and replace them with new ones.

Then start showing those new beliefs to the world.

The Belief System of the Carefree Man

Carefree Men Approach Women Just To See What Happens

Why?

Because when you're on your deathbed, you won't regret the times you got rejected. You will regret the times you never tried. You will regret the times you never got to see what happened.

Carefree men don't approach women to get anything specific from them. They don't approach to obtain some particular outcome. They approach for for only one simple reason: to see what happens.

Because seeing what happens is fun. Seeing what happens is satisfying. Seeing what happens is entertaining. And carefree men want to be entertained.

Plus, if you approach women only to see what happens, can you ever fail?

No.

Because no matter what the outcome of the interaction, the purpose has been fulfilled.

You saw what happened.

You don't spend the rest of the day kicking yourself with "what might have happened if I had just sacked up and walked over there."
That's the regret of not knowing. And it's the worst feeling in the world.

You want to know how to always avoid the pain of not knowing? Walk over there and see what happens.

It's always much more fulfilling and rewarding to see what happens. It's always much more entertaining. And no matter the outcome, it's always exhilarating.

Throughout the course we're going to start approaching women just to see what happens. When you take away the pressure of having to *get her number*, or *get a date*, or *get any particular outcome*, you're going to feel like an enormous weight has been lifted off your shoulders.

You're going to find that everything about attracting women will be so much easier.

Mental Seed #1: I approach women just to see what happens. Why? Because I don't want to die with regret. That's why.

Carefree Men Speak Without A Filter

You do this already.

Yes, you do. The problem is you only do it where it's not helpful for attracting women.

You do it at home. You do it with friends. You do it online. Some people do it in their car or in the shower (we've all seen that person having a shit-fit while sitting at the stop light).

You do it in places that feel safe. Places where you won't offend anybody. You do it when listeners are familiar or safely hidden away behind a computer screen.

Where you *don't* do it is in front of women. Particularly attractive women.

When attractive women come around, suddenly a ridiculous verbal filter appears. You start saying things that *you think* she wants to hear. You say things that *you think* will make her happy. That *you think* she won't disagree with. That *you think* will please her. That *you think* will make her attracted to you.

Then you wonder why you're not getting laid. Why women are losing interest in you and sleeping with other guys.

Well here's why. When you filter what you say, that means you are saying something you don't really believe. All the passion of saying something you believe is lost. When the passion is lost, what you're saying becomes stale, dry and boring.

Here's another word for saying something you don't really believe:

Lying.

Is that what women want? Is that who women want to sleep with? Liars?

In addition to lying, filtering makes you sound like all other guys. Because they are all lying (filtering) too. When you sound like everybody else, you don't appear different.

Make a mental note of this: **Different is interesting. Different is attractive.**

Think about it. People go to the same workplaces and watch the same shows and do the same repetitive stuff all the time. And what do they say about it?

That it's all boring (it's all boring because it's always the same).

People work and work and work at a boring job just so they can what? Go on vacation. Why is vacation interesting? Because it's different.

It's exactly the same thing with the way men talk. Hot women hear men talking all the time. When everybody sounds the same, it's boring. When a guy sounds different (i.e. telling the truth, not lying, not filtering) it's interesting.

It's attractive.

Note that different doesn't mean a purple mohawk, tattooed face and gauges the size of bowling balls.

Different just means something that stands out from the herd. Something that stands out from other guys. Even if it's subtle and a woman can't immediately identify what it is, it's still subconsciously identified.

You will see other examples of being different throughout this course. In this case, being different simply means speaking without a filter (without lying).

Now this is not a free pass to be rude to everyone. This is not saying to be an asshole. It's just saying to speak your mind about what you believe, with passion.

Here's what you're about to start noticing:

Now that you've read this, you will start noticing yourself think of something to say, and then not say it. That's filtering. That's the habit we need to break.

Here are the two main reason why people filter:

1. They think the other person will disagree.
2. They are unsure if what they are saying is correct.

Now that you're aware of the main reasons for filtering, we can start identifying when you do this, and start changing it.

Let's look further at these two reasons:

First: **It doesn't matter if she agrees with you or not.**

Disagreement is fine. Often it's good. Later in the course I'll show you exactly how to handle disagreement during a conversation.

For now just understand that her agreeing or disagreeing has no impact on whether she finds you attractive.

To fully understand that, just think about "make up sex." It's common knowledge in relationships that make-up sex is some of the best sex you can have.

And what is make-up sex? It's her disagreeing with you, and then fucking your brains out.

So...yeah...her disagreeing does not impact whether she's attracted to you or not.

Second: **It doesn't matter if what you're saying is completely accurate.**

Most of the world sits silent because they're afraid of being wrong in front of others.

You see examples of this everywhere. Think about a lecture hall in college. The professor asks a question. There's 200 people in the room. How many people volunteer answers if not specifically called upon?

Not many.

People who sit silent are not memorable. They're not different.

So here's a very important point to remember: better to speak passionately and be wrong, than to say nothing.

When it comes to women, if you say something that is wrong and she's aware it's wrong, she'll offer a different viewpoint and it's the start of a conversation.

If you just say nothing, then no conversation can happen.

Mental Seed #2: Filtering is lying. Disagreement is irrelevant. And no one ever got laid by being silent. Women are incapable of being attracted to men who filter their speech in an attempt to please them. When I speak freely, women become uncontrollably attracted to me.

Carefree Men Create Their Own Reality

You've heard stuff like this before. But what is often left out?

How.

How do you create your own reality? Do you just think about stuff?

Do you just think: *ok today I'm going to start living in a reality where I bed hot women on the daily?*

Of course not. Thinking gets you nowhere. Action gets you to your new reality.

So here's what you do. You find an actionable plan that takes you step-by-step (in achievable, bite-sized chunks) from where you are today, to your new reality.

Then you make a decision to follow that plan no matter how uncomfortable it gets.

That's exactly what this course is. And if you're reading this, then you've already started.

Props.

Mental Seed #3: As I sit here in this moment, it's hard (frankly it's almost impossible) for me to believe that I could live a life where hot chicks are calling me and trying to hook up. Regularly. A reality where hot chicks are chasing me.

I actually have no idea how I would achieve that.

But I also have found an actionable plan. A roadmap. So I'm going to commit to following every step in the process. No matter how uncomfortable it gets. I don't know what the outcome will be, but I'm going to commit anyway.

Why?

Because I just want to see what happens.

Carefree Men Give *Shit* 1 About What Other People Think -- (Carefree Men Don't Live Other People's Lives)

When you care about what other people think, you are essentially living their life. You're not living your own life. Because you are allowing their limiting beliefs to control your actions and your life.

Fully living in your new reality means that any limiting belief, thought, opinion or statement of others will become irrelevant.

A limiting belief is anything that make you hesitate. It's anything that makes you nervous about outcomes. It's anything that makes you put on a filter or bite your tongue.

It's anything that says you can't do it.

Not caring about other people's opinions is easy to say and hard to do. Because we've been conditioned by our parents and society to allow the beliefs of others to impact us.

We will tackle this fear head-on in this course. For example, later in the course you will intentionally approach chicks when other people are within earshot. When they can hear what you are doing.

That probably sounds scary as hell (probably sounds impossible) right now. But don't worry, that's not at the beginning. By the time we get there, you'll be ready.

And here's a little preview secret: You're going to learn that other people are actually impressed when they see you hitting on a hot girl.

Why?

Because they're too scared to do it themselves since, they too, are bogged down worrying about what other people think.

When they see you in action, they will wish they could do what you're doing. Often they will even congratulate you on a job well done after it's over (regardless of the outcome).

Here's another example of caring about what other people think:

People telling you that pursuing this topic is stupid. That trying to improve your game with women is a waste of time. That you should be focusing on something else.

This might come from people whose opinions you generally value. Friends and family, for example.

You need to squash those opinions directly. DO NOT just listen quietly to these people's opinions and say nothing (silence is filtering).

If these are people you generally listen to, their debilitating ideas will be clanging around in your head constantly as you work through this course. Obviously that would not be helpful to your success.

So stand up for what you believe. You don't have to be rude. But you need to remove the filter and say what you think. Tell them that creating a life that's full of sexy women is something you want. It matters to you.

If it doesn't matter to them that's fine. You're not asking them to participate. You're just telling them to get out of the way.

Smile after doing that. You'll be really happy for standing up for what you believe.

Mental Seed #4: The world doesn't care about me. The world will bombard me with its opinions, but it doesn't care if I follow those opinions and achieve a poor result. If I want something, I need to go get it. And the only opinion that matters in that journey is my own.

Carefree Men Give *Shit 1* About Rejection

There it is. The dreaded "R" word.

This is the big hurdle. **This is the biggest thing that keeps most guys living lives of quiet desperation.**

Everything else in attracting women is simple to learn and implement.

We just need to get past rejection and it's all smooth sailing. Yes, really.

AND YOU WILL GET OVER YOUR FEAR OF REJECTION IN THIS COURSE.

As long as you follow the Action Steps in Daytime Unleashed and Nighttime Unleashed.

Those supplements cover this topic in detail, so for now, let's just plant a few seeds.

All of the guys out there who you see attracting women with ease, their rejections outnumber their successes. Twice as many. Three times as many. Ten times as many.

To get to where they are now, they were uncomfortable. But they did it anyway, and rejection was just part of the process.

If you want a life filled with sexy women, you're going to encounter rejection along the way. There's no way around it. So just accept it. Embrace it.

Rejection is not a failure. Rejection is just another example of seeing what happens.

Here's the secret:

It's not a simple "rejection" that guys are afraid of. A simple rejection is just "sorry I have a boyfriend" or "I'm flattered but I'm not interested." There's nothing really scary about that.

What guys are scared of is the *mean rejection*, the *rude rejection*, the *humiliating rejection*.

They're scared of that because it probably happened to them once back in junior high or high school. Back when kids were just assholes. Or they've seen movies where some nerd asks out a hot cheerleader and suddenly 10 sorority girls are all laughing and pointing.

And they have projected that one experience, or that one ridiculous scene from a movie, onto how "all rejections" are going to be. Literally that one experience or scene has road-blocked them from even approaching women.

How awful.

The reality is that this almost never happens. **In most cases women are flattered to be approached**. Even if they turn you down, they are flattered. You can literally make a womans day by hitting on her. REALLY.

If a woman is going to put *that much* effort into looking so good. It is your obligation, YOU OWE IT TO HER, to walk over there and say something.

OK, occasionally you might get an eye roll and get ignored. So what.....

You will most likely have a long, successful life approaching women, and some horrendous, high school, movie-style rejection is NEVER going to happen.

If it happens, it's like getting struck by lightning.

Are you never going to go outside because of that one tiny chance you might get struck by lightning?

Mental Seed #5: Rejection happens. Fuck it.

Bonus Tip On Rejection And Caring About What Other People Think

Some people in this course are starting at the very beginning of attracting women -- essentially just working on improving basic social skills.

Because of that I want to add two important points about rejection and caring what other people think.

Internalize these statements and you'll start to see that all your energy wasted on worrying about rejection and other people's opinions is ridiculous.

- The only person who remembers a rejection is you.
- Most of the time, people aren't thinking anything about you. At all.

One of the biggest problems I've encountered with guys just starting out improving their social skills is this:

There's this lingering, painful belief (again, probably left over from junior high and high school) that: "everyone is talking about you."

That: "everyone is thinking something about you."

That if you were rejected: "everyone would know it and be laughing at you."

To start eliminating these beliefs, ask yourself this question:

What are you thinking about them?

The answer is probably *nothing*. Or it's just you thinking that they are thinking something about you. How convoluted.

The truth is that people don't have time to worry about you. They don't have the time or the interest to care if you get rejected. **No one cares about you.**

Don't take that as an insult. <u>Take it as a pleasant feeling of relief</u>.

No one has 5 seconds to spare in our busy world to "talk about you" and to "think about you."

If you get rejected, nobody knows or cares or remembers, except you.

Think about it. How many guys have you seen get rejected, and now *you* are thinking about them getting rejected, and talking about it with other people?

None.

So stop worrying about that shit.

Let's do an experiment.

Imagine you're in a room where the lights are dim. You're sitting on one side of the room with a clipboard and pen. On the other side there are 10 women lined up.

You can see them only from the neck up. Pretend there's a wall blocking the rest of their bodies. All of them have shaved heads and shaved eyebrows. They have on no makeup. Their eyes are closed. Their mouths are closed. The expression of their lips is flat and blank.

Then the lights come on.

You now have 20 seconds to put the women in order from most attractive to least attractive. Essentially you have 2 seconds per face to make a decision.

And what is the only thing you really have available to judge? Bone structure. That's pretty much it. All other variables have been stripped away.

Now imagine that the experiment is conducted again with the same 10 women.

However this time they are all dolled up, ready for the club. We're talking high heels, makeup, hair from the salon, cleavage busting out everywhere, legs for days, you name it. Also, there's no wall this time to block the view.

The lights come on and you have 20 seconds to put them in order.

Afterwards the two lists are compared.

Do you think that the ordering of the women on the two lists is going to be the same?

Most certainly not.

The girl you ranked #1 for facial structure could have wound up with #10 after you saw her rocking *bootydoo* (you know...that's where her stomach sticks out further than her booty do).

Meanwhile, #10 for facial structure could have a body that is literally oozing sex from every opening in that skimpy little dress. She's dripping with confidence, banging hot, and she knows it.

The reality is that any resemblance between the two lists would be coincidental.

This thought exercise demonstrates that only a tiny fraction of "what you look like" has to do with your facial structure.

Most of "what you look like" has to do with: posture, body language, the confidence with which you carry yourself, physical fitness, clothes, haircut, and how your facial hair is shaved. All things that are within your control.

Even your teeth, eye color and skin tone are within your control.

The only thing that is out of your control is bone structure.

But ironically, that's the very thing most guys are referring to when they fall victim to: Women Are Only Attracted To "Good Looking Guys."

They are associating "good looking" with bone structure.

Now imagine the above experiment conducted with 10 men. You don't need to think through the details this time. By now it should be clear that what a man looks like, what you look like, has almost nothing to do with your bone structure. It has everything to do with variables that you can control.

So let's be very clear.

Women care about what you look like.

But "what you look like" has very little to do with your facial bone structure and very much to do with all the other factors within your control.

Here's the reason guys still associate "what you look like" with bone structure.

Some time, long ago, they were told that they were ugly. This was back when they were kids and "all the other factors" really weren't in their control.

That's because when they were kids, their mom picked out their clothes. Their mom decided their haircut. Maybe they had zits and mom wouldn't buy them acne cream.

Whatever.

Because everything was out of their control, they made the association that "ugly" basically means their face (or more specifically, bone structure).

And because they were now convinced they were ugly, they never took control of all the other factors once they became adults. They never got in shape. They wear shitty clothes. They have bad haircuts. Maybe they still have acne, because....well, no point in fixing that when everything else is a mess.

So they have allowed all the other factors to fall apart and the entire package looks like shit. To fix that, it's time to take control of all the other factors….

Mental Seed #6: What You "Look Like" Breaks Down Like This:

- 50% is how you carry yourself. It's the confidence you exude in how you talk, stand, walk, and sit. It's your body language. It's the smirk on your face. It's the tone of your voice. It's the fire burning in your eyes. It's the confidence of locking eyes with a really hot chick at the bar and walking over there with no hesitation. Walking over there while all the "good looking guys" are standing around waiting for the buzz to kick in so they have the confidence to do something. This 50% is completely within your control.

- 25% is your body fitness. It's the muscles in your arms, shoulders, stomach, chest and back. It's the confidence that comes from lifting. It's the confidence that comes from the way women look at your body when you pass by (the look that says: "yum, yum, yuuuum"). This 25% is also completely within your control. And the best part is, you don't need to be a bodybuilder. You just need to get off your ass and start pumping some weight. More on this later.

-   25% is your face. However as we said before, your haircut, the way you shave your beard, your skin, your teeth, even the color of your eyes are all within your control. Only a small percentage relates to your bone structure. And that part doesn't matter. Get all the other variables under control, and women will find you sexy as hell.

Mental Seed # 6: I control what I look like. No excuses.

Carefree Guys Know That Money Has Nothing To Do With Attraction

Are there sugar babies in the world? Yes. Are there golddiggers? Yes. So doesn't that mean that women are attracted to money?

To correctly answer that, let's change the question to be as specific as possible.

Are women sexually attracted to money? In other words, do women feel an uncontrollable tingling between their legs if they find out a guy has money.

The answer to that is 100% no.

However, can nice guys and beta males get women to hang around them if they have money?

Sure.

Some women are happy to have these guys buy them drinks and fancy dinners and expensive gifts. Maybe even take them on trips. Maybe pay their bills. And will they sleep with these guys after all this stuff?

Sure. At least sometimes. Hell, sometimes she'll even marry them.

So let's be clear. There are definitely some women out there who are attracted to money. But that doesn't mean they are <u>sexually attracted</u> to the man holding the money.

Nothing about money sparks primal, uncontrollable, panty dripping, sexual attraction.

You don't need money to create that.

What you need to do is (1) ingrain the Carefree Man Belief System into your soul and (2) implement the single secret to attracting women which you will learn about in the next chapter.

Spoiler: The secret has nothing to do with money.

Mental Seed #7: Money is not sexually attractive. Lack of money is an excuse I will never use again. Forget the golddiggers. There are an unlimited number of hot, sexy women out there that I will attract once I start showing the Carefree Man belief system to the world.

Carefree Guys Have The Delusional Belief That All Women Want Them...Badly

You may be scratching your head on this one, saying: *I can't see myself believing that. I can't just believe that all women want me...badly.*

If you're saying that right now, then guess what? It's not just *right now*. It's all the time.

You are currently walking through this world with essentially the opposite belief: that women don't want you.

That belief is reflected in your demeanor, your confidence, your body language, your aura, everything. That belief is oozing out of you whether you know it or not. (Again, you've made the choice to project this opposite belief to the world).

And when women see a guy who projects to the world that no women want him, guess what happens?

They don't want him either.

The world will accept whatever you project. That's the second thing I want you to write on a sticky note and post on your bathroom mirror.

If you project that you're a loser and no women want you, the world will accept that.

If you project that you have the delusional belief that all women want you, badly. The world will start to accept that too.

That's the Law of Assumption. When you assume something (anything, it doesn't have to be about women), everything about your body, mind and soul will project that to the world. And the world will start to accept it.

Think about a confident guy walking down the street with his head held high and a fire burning in his eyes. The kind of guy who looks at women with the look that says "I know you want me." Basically a really attractive guy.

What is he projecting to the world? That women want him. And guess what...they do.

Right now you're probably assuming and projecting to the world that women DON'T find you attractive. And guess what...they don't.

Think about it.

You've heard the statement: *assuming makes an ass out of you and me.* Let's change that statement to reflect the new reality you are building.

Mental Seed #8: Assuming gets me ass and even more puss-e.

Final note on this. Carefree guys also assume that everybody is crazy interested to know what they are thinking about and talking about. (And not in a *judging them* way that we tossed out earlier under rejection and what other people thing. But rather in a *wow, you're such an interesting person, I'm deathly curious about whatever it is going on in your mind. Please bestow your knowledge on me, kind of way*).

You will see this assumption come up a lot later in the conversation sections of this course.

That's the belief system of the Carefree Man. Throughout the course we're going to make those ideas grow until they become your own and you naturally project them to the world.

When that happens, you will be unstoppable with women.

Chapter 2: 25 Day Action Plan to Change Your Life

The Action Steps that make up the 25 Day Action Plan to Change Your Life are found in your two bonus supplement guides:

- Daytime Unleashed
- Nighttime Unleashed

The supplements are designed to be used in conjunction with this course.

The Action Steps in the supplements are CRITICAL to your success. As I've said, if you just read this course and don't do the action steps, nothing is going to happen.

The Action Steps should be done in order.

Start with Daytime Unleashed and then move to Nighttime Unleashed.

Trust me. If you power through these action steps no matter how scary they are, it will change your life.

The Action Steps start off very easy and then get progressively harder. Don't bother reading past the Action Step which has been assigned. Do the assigned one. When complete come back to this guide and keep reading.

This guidebook will tell you when to stop reading and which Action Step to go complete.

Just like this:

Stop reading now. Go to Daytime Unleashed. Read and complete Action Step 1.

Then come back here and pick up with Chapter 3.

(Really….don't keep reading. For the words below to truly change your life, you need the dopamine rush, that will come from completing the Action Step, to be coursing through your veins. Without the dopamine, it's just a bunch words. Your choice.)

Chapter 3: How Women Work, The Secret All Guys Want

Women Are Not Logical & Attraction Is Not Linear

Understanding this is critical to your success. Giving women logical, rational reasons why they should be attracted to you will get you nowhere.

This is why women are not attracted to "nice guys." It would be logical to be attracted to a nice guy. Women will even say they "want a nice guy." They say that because it sounds logical. But that's not really what they want.

Let's be more specific. In the office and at school, women can be logical. But when it comes to attraction. When it comes to seduction, women are not logical.

They are emotional.

Logical reasoning is linear (i.e. first you do A, then B, then C, etc).

Emotional reasoning is not linear.

Listen up:

A good looking guy, with a good job, but no idea how to create a positive emotional reaction in a woman, can give some girl the most logical, methodical explanation as to why he would be the best candidate for her affection.

And she will sit there, bored to tears, thinking about nothing more than how she can get away from this guy.

A less attractive guy, with no job, who sleeps on a basement couch, but knows how to rip through her soul with a fucking tsunami off fun, positive, and challenging emotions, doesn't even have to show interest in her. In fact, he can even playfully tell her he's not interested.

And she will be fascinated by this guy. She will go to bed thinking about him. She will dream about him. And she will absolutely find a way into his bedroom (or couch in this example) and fight off other girls to get there.

That's not a joke.

The reason it may *seem* like a joke is because it's not logical. There is nothing logical about the picture I just painted for you.

But that's the way it is.

The takeaways from this section are as follows:

- When you have conversations with women, you will sometimes say things that are not logical, especially at the beginning (you will see exactly how to do this in the examples later). What you say may not be logical, but it will be fun, positive and challenging.

- When you have conversations with women, you will not stick to a logical order. Fun, positive and challenging conversations can start anywhere, and will switch from topic to topic regularly and without warning.

*****

There is one exception to be aware of before we move on. One *logical* thing which must be overcome when seducing a woman is this:

Are You Safe?

Other than *are you safe*, everything else is emotional.

We'll cover how to overcome the *are you safe* issue throughout the course.

Fun, Positive & Challenging Emotions

Everything in this course is about changing **YOU**, so you can deliver the tsunami of fun, positive and challenging emotions that women can't resist.

Deliver them naturally, powerfully and instantly, at the flip of a switch.

And, **VERY IMPORTANT**: So you can take them away. Instantly. At the same flip of the switch.

That's it. Right there.

That's the secret that guys search for their entire lives. **Fill her with fun, positive and challenging emotions. Then take them away. Over and over.**

Fun, positive and challenging emotions are like an attraction drug. And what happens when you take a drug away from an addict?

They will do anything to get more.

Everything you will ever hear about in seduction; everything you will see throughout this course; everything you will ever see ANYWHERE about this topic, is just some version of the secret above.

This course is about transforming you into a man who does that. Naturally. Without thinking about it.

Once you are that version of yourself, women will be chasing you down.

Women's Emotions Are Affected By Their Surroundings

You've probably noticed that women like to decorate. Stores around the world have shelves lined floor-to-ceiling with decorative stuff targeted at women.

Women are constantly trying to "perfect" their surroundings because of this emotional impact.

But surroundings doesn't just mean curtains, vases, rugs, candles and incense. Surroundings also means people. And in the case of attracting women into your life, people means YOU.

When you are talking to a woman, YOU are impacting her emotional state. That's why we are going to transform you into a man who **fills her with fun, positive and challenging emotions.**

Women Are Attracted To Guys Who Go For What They Want

Going for what you want means you are interested in the world. You're not afraid to take risks. You have passions and dreams.

The more you go after what you want, the more attractive you become.

And in the conversation sections of this course, we're going to learn all about how to express your interests, passions and dreams to her as you ramp up the attraction.

Going for what you want also means approaching her with confidence and without hesitation. However, very important:

Getting her cannot be the only thing you want. If that's all you want, you will quickly become smothering to her. So when you approach her without hesitation, you need to subsequently give her the feeling that you can (and very well might) walk away without hesitation.

Everything is giving and taking away. Pushing and pulling. Reaching and withdrawing. Having other interests, passions and dreams, and being able to express those things to her allows you to "withdraw" from simply being interested in *getting her*.

In your bonus supplement 7 Mental Exercises To Get You Laid, we're going to cover how to be prepared to express these passions and dreams to her.

Women Think About Sex All The Time Too

Women are horny creatures. Just like men. Society really tries hard to convince you that this is not true. But it is 100% true.

A few months ago I was flying home from a mastermind group. The plane had just landed. You know that moment when the plane finally gets to the jetway, there's a ding, and every unbuckles and stands up? It was that moment.

I stood up, but of course the aisle is jammed and I'm going nowhere. The guy in front of me doesn't stand up. So as I'm standing there waiting for all the slowpokes to move (you always wonder don't you -- have these people ever deplaned before???) the guy in front of me pulls out his phone, as everyone does.

He goes to his messages and texts "I'm home," to a female name. OK I probably shouldn't have been text-spying on him, but whatever.

So a message comes back. It wasn't long, but it made me smile because it proved the point I'm always trying explain to guys (why guys don't believe this, I'm not sure).

The message said: "thank God cuz I need to be fucked so bad"

The point is: women are horny. They're going to fuck someone. Your job is to make yourself the kind of man that they pick over someone else.

The Female Attraction Formula

The formula to attract women is simple.

- Phase 1: Smash or Pass
- Phase 2: Curiosity
- Phase 3: Fascination
- Phase 4: Captivation

There is a chapter dedicated to each of these 4 phases coming up. I'm going to show you in excruciating detail **HOW** to do this (everything from what to say to how to move your body).

For now, let's go through each phase high level. Also note that the names of these phases doesn't matter. Don't get too hung up on what I've called them. They simply represent the level of emotional investment she has made in you.

Let's dive into that further.

Phase 1 - Smash or Pass. In this Phase she's made zero emotional investment in you. This phase is really brief. A couple seconds. It's basically, when she first sees you, do you meet the fundamental criteria for a potential sexual partner.

Fundamental criteria doesn't mean that you're the "best looking" guy in the room. It just means: is your grooming in order? Do you have all the variables about "what you look like" under control? If you do, then you are simply *not dismissed* as a potential sexual partner.

Phase 2 – Curiosity: This is the first few minutes of you talking with each other. Here she is starting to experience fun, positive and challenging emotions from you. If you're delivering these emotions correctly, she's becoming curious about you.

In this phase she's making a low emotional investment in you. Low emotional investment means that the conversation is generally limited to topics that don't involve each person revealing anything too deep or personal (don't worry, we will cover how to make conversation like this ad nauseum in later chapters).

This is the phase where you will begin touching her on certain "public" areas of her body (for example, fist bumps, high fives, upper back). See your bonus supplement How To Touch Women for comprehensive examples of how this works.

Phase 3 – Fascination: In this phase she continues to experience fun, positive and challenging emotions. She starts wondering if you are actually a real, genuine, no filter guy, or if she's just dreaming.

In this phase she starts making a high emotional investment in you -- i.e. the conversation turns to topics that require her to reveal more personal things about herself. This phase also involves you revealing more personal information about yourself.

The conversation is deeper and an emotional connection begins to develop between the two of you.

This is the stage where she really starts pondering if you could be an actual sexual partner. Like not just in theory, but for real.

Phase 4 – Captivation: This is the phase where she's highly attracted to you. It's time to close the deal.

Stop here. Go to Daytime Unleashed and Complete Action Step #2. Then return and pick up in Chapter 4.

Chapter 4: Attraction Phase 1 - Smash or Pass

Have you seen the smash or pass game on Youtube?

If not, it's very simple. The host of the video approaches a girl or a group of girls, shows them pictures of guys, and asks them: "smash or pass?"

Smash or pass basically means: would you sleep with this guy based solely on what you see in the picture?

EVERYONE is playing the smash or pass game in their head, all day, everyday.

You play it all the time. Every time you see a women and you're mind says "damn…" That means *smash*. When you see bootydoo, *pass*.

And how long does it take to make that decision? About 2 seconds. Literally the time it takes for your eyes to give her a quick *up-n-down*. Decision made.

Does this sound familiar?

Does this sound like the thought experiment we performed earlier in Make Women Chase You? The one with the 10 women - bald headed vs. dressed for the club.

And what did we determine at the end of that experiment? That what you look like IS important. But what you look like has little to do with your facial bone structure, and everything to do with variables within your control.

Well women are playing the smash or pass game too. All day, everyday. And they are certainly playing it with men who approach them with sexual interest.

So here's how the smash or pass game works out in real life:

- A smash decision means that based on what you look like (again almost completely within your control), are you a potential sex partner. That doesn't mean she's going to have sex with you. It just means you're not immediately and permanently dismissed. That's the first hurdle.
- A pass decision means you're immediately and permanently dismissed. Once this happens, she might still talk to you for a minute, but it's pretty much over.

So to get a smash decision, we need take charge of all the variables we can control.

Always Be Ready - If keeping yourself fresh and groomed regularly isn't a habit, you need to make it a habit starting immediately. If you don't, it's very easy to let hot women walk by using the excuse of "I wasn't ready." That's a bullshit excuse.

Starting today you need to always be ready. Leave the house everyday with the intention of approaching women. And being groomed and ready to approach. Even if you're just going out to run errands.

This doesn't mean you have to approach every women you see. It just means you'll be ready when a hottie appears right in front of you. Because for some reason, hotties always seem to appear when you're "not ready." So from now on, always be ready.

Hair - Have a fresh, crisp haircut. Ideally one that best fits your face. There's tons of information out there to help you with this. Google this topic or find a good barber and have them figure it out. Believe me that a good haircut can dramatically impact "what you look like." At a minimum, just make sure you have a fresh trim.

Beard - If you're gonna shave, be freshly shaved. If you look good with a 5 o'clock shadow, take advantage of that. I know lots of guys that rock the 5 o'clock. Here's the key. Make sure the 5 o'clock looks *intentional*. Not like you were just lazy and didn't shave. How? Shave all around the edges of the 5 o'clock. Shave off the bottom ½ inch of the neck-line so there is a crisp line separating the 5 o'clock from the rest of your neck. Shave the lines on the cheek so they are crisp. Shave any stragglers at the top of the mustache (just under the nose). Lots of facial hair styles can look great -- as long as they look like you did it on purpose (not just that you're unshaven).

If you rock a beard, take some time to learn about grooming styles. How you groom your beard can have a dramatic impact on what you look like. You can actually groom to make your chin look more prominent. How? Here's the basics:

Think of your beard in 3 sections: the goatee (section a), the sideburns straight down to the jaw (section c), and the section in between those two (section b). Let's say your razor has 3 shaving lengths from 1 to 3, with 3 being the longest. You start by shaving your entire beard with a 3 (the longest). Then you shave everything except the goatee (section a) using a 2 (the middle length). Then you shave the sideburns section (section c) with a 1 (the shortest length).

This makes your beard fade from short to middle to long as you look from ear to chin. That creates the illusion of you having a longer, more pronounced jaw and chin.

Any visible ear and nose hair - removed.

Fingernails - short and clean under the nail.

Fragrance - obviously you should be showered, clean and deodorized. Hit yourself with 2 squirts of an expensive cologne. I like one squirt on upper body and a second on the crotch. Because who knows, that second squirt could be useful later.

Poor man's hack: if you're a broke college dude, swing by the mall before any hot date, go to the fragrance section in a department store, and hit yourself with the testers.

Oral Hygiene - Brush your teeth. Pop a tic tac. A lot of people find chewing gum just makes them feel more confident. It's a strange phenomenon. Try it out. Plus women always ask if they can have a piece of gum. Which you can give them, but only with conditions that they do something for you (more on handling tests coming up soon).

Clothes - This is where a lot of guys get hung up. And fashion advice can be a book in and of itself. And what looks good will be different for everybody. So let's keep it simple.

The best fashion for you is clean, crisp, fresh looking clothes that you are comfortable in. Whatever you can wear that makes you feel the most confident, that's the best choice for now.

In general stick to solid neutral colors. Don't be too "loud" with your clothes, unless you are intentionally peacocking.

Differentiator - You should have between 1 and 3 unique differentiators. These are generally watches, bracelets, necklaces, rings and earrings. The choice and style will vary depending on your personality and what makes you comfortable. But trust me, I've seen guys with ears full of rings having women falling all over them. So anything can work, when you make it work.

Ideally any differentiator should have a little story associated with it. Or it should have some meaning or significance to you (like you got it on some trip, or someone important gave it to you). This is because a differentiator is a common thing to come up in initial conversation with a woman. She will notice it, might point it out, and ask about it. So have something to say about it.

If you literally can't think of anything to say about your differentiator, you can just tell her: "cuz it looks good" (confident wink, confident smirk).

Don't overlook the differentiator. Get at least one. It's important to make you subtly stand out from the crowd.

Body language - Here's the basics:

When you're walking -- Walk with intention and purpose. Walk slowly. Don't scurry like a little mouse. Walk around like you own the place. Walk into a room like you own the place. Walk around like you're the baddest ass motherfucker in the world. Because in your world, you are the baddest ass motherfucker. So act like it.

When you sit -- Open up. Uncross your legs. Uncross your arms. Take up more space. Sit in a way that takes up as much space as possible.

When you stand -- Legs open at shoulder width. Back straight. Head held high. Hands out of your pockets. Or if in your pockets, thumbs out. Don't put your entire hand in your pocket.

Eye movements - slow and intentional. Keep your eyes from flickering and fluttering. Make strong eye contact with women. This doesn't mean stare. It means if you make eye contact with a women, look at her like a fucking man. Don't let your eyes pull away because you're scared. Look at her like you know everything she could possible say. Look at her like you're the keeper of her soul.

Head movements - Slow and intentional. No head jerking. No head bobbling. You don't need to head bobble in agreement with everything people say. Just look at them with a smirk.

Slow down everything you do. Really, slow down. Talk slower. Walk slower. Chew slower. Put your fork down on the table between bites. Turn your head to look at things slower. Answer slower. Pause for dramatic effect.

Have a deep voice. To this one you may be saying: *you can't change your voice. You can't make yourself have a deep voice. People try that and actually hurt their vocal cords.* Well here's the secret of a deep voice: Slow down. That's it. Slow your talking down. The faster you talk, the more your voice will uncontrollably rise in pitch. So slow it down.

All of the grooming items above are critical from Day 1. So read over the list again if necessary and get these things in order.

For body language, start by improving one thing. If it's walking with slow intention and purpose (walking like you own the place), then consciously practice improving that everywhere you go. Spend a week on it. Do it until it feels natural. Then pick something else. Focus some energy on these things and you will master them. Then it will be natural and you won't need to think about doing it.

Chapter 5: Attraction Phase 2 - Curiosity

Congratulations! You've arrived at the most exciting part of this course. This is where we really start approaching and talking to women.

We've discussed that approach anxiety may be the largest issue holding men back. But underlying the fear of approaching is really the fear of getting stuck in awkward silences and not knowing what to say.

If you always know what to say, or have a strategy to easily keep conversations going, then approaching women becomes so much simpler and more comfortable.

In this chapter we are going to talk in depth about how to start conversations and keep them going.

Let's begin.

How To Start Conversations & Keep Them Going

Assumptions

Assumptions are a great way to spark curiosity. Imagine if someone was randomly like:

"Hey, you're from Texas aren't you?"

You'd be like: "No. Why do you think that?"

You'd be curious why they thought that. Having something assumed about you sparks curiosity in a natural, almost knee-jerk way. Without even thinking about it, you just ask why someone thinks or asks that.

It works the same way with women. If you just assume something about them, they will be curious why you thought that.

The great thing about assumptions is they can relate to anything. The most common starters would be assumptions about her name, where she's from, what she does for fun, where she goes to school, what she likes to drink, what music she likes, etc.

The topics can be all the same as questions you might ask when meeting a person. But instead of 'what's your name,' it's 'you name is [blank], isn't it.' Or instead of 'where are you from?' it's "You're from [blank] aren't you?"

You're going after the same information as you would when starting any conversation. The only difference is that instead of asking a question to kick things off, you assume something.

Assumptions are incredibly easy because they don't need to be right. In fact, they should generally be wrong. If you see a chick wearing full yoga gear and you assume 'hey, you're a yoga girl aren't you?' it's not nearly as interesting as 'hey, you're a rock climber aren't you?'

So generally we will make assumptions about women that are wrong. We'll do lots examples of this coming up.

Tactic Arsenal

I want you to think of assumptions and all the other techniques we're going to discuss as tools in an arsenal.

Not every tool is right for every situation. You don't need to use every tool all the time, and you don't need to use a tool every time you speak. That would just make you seem like a pain in the ass.

For example, if you were talking to someone and all you did was make assumptions, it would be really annoying.

So the point of the tools is to sprinkle them in throughout the conversation. Once you master enough tools, you'll be able to mix all these techniques up, which will make everything flow naturally.

Nicknames

Nicknames create a small emotional connection between people. It's also a great topic of discussion -- like: "so what was your embarrassing childhood nickname?" Or if you're making an assumption: "i bet your embarrassing childhood nickname was [blank]."

That can lead to not only getting the nickname, but the story associated with it. In turn, you might share your embarrassing childhood nickname with her.

If childhood nicknames don't come up, then giving the girl a nickname during the conversation (based on information you find out about her) is also great.

Cliffhangers

Fun conversations have cliffhangers. They leave an open conversational thread which can be returned to later (a great way to keep conversations going when a stopping point for another topic has been reached).

We will refer to these as cliffhangers, unclosed loops, or unclosed conversation threads.

Because the conversational thread is open, it also creates some mystery because she may have wanted to know more about it, but you've already moved on to something else.

Cliffhangers also allow conversations to be nonlinear because they come from abruptly ending one topic, moving to another, and then returning to the first topic at some point later.

Creating cliffhangers is closely related to the next topic, changing the subject.

Changing The Subject

This is one of the best tactics for keeping conversations going.

If you become great at one thing during this course it's going to be changing the subject.

We're going to talk about this a lot. Changing the subject allows you never to get stuck during a conversation, because you can (and should) randomly change to something else.

You do it right in the middle of some conversational thread. And that creates a cliffhanger which can be returned to later.

Have you ever noticed that women are usually great multitaskers. That's because their mind moves from topic to topic in a quick, non-linear fashion. That's how their mind works and is another reason why logical conversations don't spark attraction.

You will see lots of examples of changing the subject coming up.

Why We Never Ask Questions This Way Again

Starting conversations and keeping conversations going is the biggest problem guys have with women.

Some would argue that "approach" or "approach anxiety" is the biggest problem. But one of the fundamental reasons why "approach" is so hard is because guys aren't' sure what to say and are afraid of getting stuck in awkward silences. This is usually more of a concern than flat out rejection.

So we're going to talk about "what to say" and "how to keep the conversation going" a lot. Starting now.

Let's start with three of the most basic topics that will be part of any "getting to know you" conversation.

- What's your name?
- Where are you from?
- What do you do for fun?

You should NEVER ask these questions in this format again.

Why?

Two reasons.

First, because it's boring. Everybody asks questions this way. And as we've been discussing, doing something different sparks curiosity simply because it's different.

The second reason is that a boring question leads to a short, boring answer. Usually an answer that doesn't provide an easy transition to further discussion.

In that case, usually guys just ask another boring question. Then they get another boring answer. And the conversation turns into a boring and uncomfortable question and answer session. Which I assure you makes her bored out of her mind.

So let's change this: Let's change to starting conversations off with an assumption (a guess), as often as is possible.

Instead of: "what's your name?"

Say: "You're name is Amber isn't it?"

This sparks curiosity. Why would you say that?

The most common response to this is something like:

"No. Why would you think that?"
"It's Jenny. But what makes you say that?"

You're response is something like:

"I don't know…...you just look like an Amber to me."
"I'm not sure…...you're just giving me that Amber vibe."
"I'm not sure…….there's just something about you."

You should look curious, like you're really pondering it.

Like: *what is it that makes this girl look like an Amber.* You should have a curious smirk on your face.

Hold for one or two beats, pondering, then move on (comprehensive examples coming up.)

By moving on and changing the subject, you've left a cliffhanger. Because the fact that something caused you to think her name was Amber is still sitting out there. You haven't revealed *WHY* you though that yet.

That's an unclosed loop which will keep her wondering.

When it comes to assumptions, women are like elephants; they never forget. Even if you're further along in the conversation at this point, she has not forgotten that you looked at her and thought her name was Amber.

And she will *HAVE TO* find out why. Women can't help wanting to know why people think things about them.

Also, this is another example of being non-linear. You said she looks like an Amber. You said there was something about her. And then you moved on to something else instead of finishing this conversation thread. That's non-linear.

You will see an immediate increase in attraction from women when you learn to change the subject (i.e. bounce around non-linearly, with your conversation).

Keeping Conversations Going

<u>Cliffhangers Are Not "One-Time" Events</u>

It's always great to find one cliffhanger and drag it out. That simply means that you are dragging the suspense out. You are deferring your answer.

Again, you don't use every tactic all the time. Imagine if all you did was drop cliffhangers and then just never answered anything and drug out the suspense forever. That would make you a true pain in the ass. So use moderation. Sprinkle it in.

Dragging out cliffhangers is also a great tactic when you really don't have a reason (or haven't come up with one yet).

For example, assume you said: "I don't know......you just look like an Amber to me."

Now assume that she's really interested at this moment, and she's pressing you for more information. Who knows, maybe her sister's name is Amber and it's really weird that you said that and not only does she *HAVE TO* know, but she has to know *NOW*.

You just keep deferring (with a playful smirk and tone, as always).

"I'm gonna have to think about it."
"I'm not sure, there's something though."
"I'll have to think about it and i'll tell you later."

Then you change the subject (move on). Here's an example:

Name Example

You: "You're name is Amber isn't it?"
Her: "It's Jenny. But what makes you say that?"
You: "I don't know…...you just look like an Amber to me."
You: "What about your middle name? Is that Amber?"
Her: "Nope. Jenny Elizabeth Henderson."
You: "Hmmm….well, good to meet you Jenny Elizabeth Henderson. I'm Mark Thomas Parker. But my friends call me Shaggy."
(you two shake hands).
Her: "(hopefully giggling) Why do they call you Shaggy?
(what do we do here? Answer the question? No -- we defer. Leave cliffhangers).
 You: "Wait a second. You think I'm gonna tell you the *history* of the Shagster when you haven't even shared *your* nickname? Com'on. Cough it up. What was your embarrassing childhood nickname?"
Her: "(blushing) I can't tell you."

You: "Pshhht…(looking away)... looks like we can't be drinking buddies anymore Jenny Elizabeth Henderson.

Her: "If I tell you, you can't laugh."

You: "I won't…...the Shagster might...but I won't.

Her: "Forget it lol! (maybe punches you in the shoulder)".

You: "Ok seriously. Pinky swear (you take her hand - yes touching - and do a pinky swear). See. The oath has been taken. The Shagster will not laugh."

Her: "(hesitant) It was Peaches."

You: (you are now non-reactive for a few beats -- you don't do anything, just look at her after she revealed the secret. Then after a few moments of tension building, you act like that's the dumbest thing you've ever heard. Don't laugh, because you swore not to. But close your eyes. Smack your forehead with the palm of your hand. Put your head in your hands. Shake your head. -- remember ALL PLAYFULLY).

Her: "Stop it! You swore not to laugh. (maybe punches your shoulder again)"

You: "(still trying to recover from you disappointment) I'm not….I'm not laughing…..I...

…..just…...PEACHES? (repeat the name with emphasis) Your name was PEACHES? (then playfully-sarcastic) That's the cutest thing I've ever heard."

Her: "Alright Shagster...it's your turn. Spill it."

You: (and now you move into telling a story)

Let's break it down.

First. How much longer and more interesting was this conversation than:

Question: What's your name?
Answer: Jenny.

This was a full minute of fun, playful conversation. You may have even touched her 3 times. The handshake. The pinky swear. And the punches to the shoulder (if you were lucky enough to get some).

And the best part, we haven't even gotten past names and nicknames yet. And with the story of the Shagster coming up (naturally followed by the story of Peaches), there's easily another 1 to 2 minutes of conversation left to be had, just on this topic.

Second. Let's look at "But my friends call me Shaggy." Now obviously you don't need to use Shaggy. Use whatever nickname you really had as a kid (and have a really funny story prepared about the nickname -- see your bonus: 7 Mental Exercises To Get You Laid.)

What did this line do? It sparked curiosity. Telling anybody that your nickname is [whatever] is going to spark curiosity. Then when you tell the story about the nickname, it creates a small emotional connection. Why?

Because the story will most certainly involve mom or family members or friends or camp counselors or whatever. And since she has all of those people in her life too, it's a topic you can both relate to.

When you can both relate to something, that creates an emotional connection.

And randomly telling her that is an example of another important tactic for keeping conversations going:

Tell Her Something About Yourself

You can always tell her something random about yourself. Something that will spark curiosity.

Just blurt it out.

A nickname is a great one that you can use in every conversation you have with a woman for the rest of your life. But you can literally say anything:

You: "What about your middle name? Is that Amber?"
Her: "Nope. Jenny Elizabeth Henderson."
You: "Hmmm....well, good to meet you Jenny Elizabeth Henderson. I'm Mark Thomas Parker. (you two shake hands).
You: "Well, since I had no luck guessing your name, I'll just tell you something about myself. Last week I went skydiving for the first time.

- Last week I joined a yoga class. Now look me up and down and tell me, what about me looks like a "yoga guy."
- Last week I moved here from Cincinnati. You're my first date (wink).
- Last week I took a class on how to make sushi. And I accidently sliced off the tip of my latex glove, which ended up in the spicy salmon roll I was making. And then the instructor came around to sample the rolls. And.........

The point is that it can be anything. And it can (and should be) something random. It does not have to be a logical thing. It does not have to be a logical transition (names to skydiving or Cincinnati or sushi rolls….whatever).

You can even skip the "Well since I had no luck guessing…." part:

- I'm Mark Thomas Parker and I'm a yogaholic
- I'm a sushiholic
- I spend 3 hours a day writing copy for [whatever] magazine
- I spend 2 hours a day under the hood of classic cars
- I spend my Saturdays teaching underprivileged youth to do [whatever]

It can be anything randomly thrown in after you introduce yourself. It should be something that random and playful and sparks curiosity.

Baby Step Topic Changes

So now we've seen an example of assumptions, cliffhangers and changing the subject.

But let's be very clear about changing the subject. It does not have to be dramatic. It does not have to be names to Cincinnati. It can be small. In the original example it started with guessing her first hame. Then guessing a middle name. Then going to nicknames.

Similar topics are still topic changes.

Dynamic Nicknames

Once you get her childhood nickname (or give her a nickname based on information you learn about her), don't keep it static.

Use any variation you want. In this example, as the conversation went on through the night, you can refer to her as any of these: peaches; peachster; peachmeister; peach cobbler; peachy; peachy keen; Peaches Henderson; lil Miss Peach, and dozens more.

What If She Doesn't Have A Nickname?

You: "Wait a second. You think I'm gonna tell you the history of the Shagster when you haven't even told me your nickname? Com'on. Cough it up. What was your embarrassing childhood nickname?"

Her: "I never had one."

You: "Pshhht…(looking away)… looks like we can't be drinking buddies anymore Jenny Elizabeth Henderson.

Her: "No seriously. I never had one."

You: "(looking skeptical) You've got to be kidding. Your mom never called you *sweet pea* or *sugarplum* or *freckle butt*?

Her: "Swear. Nothing like that. My mom was very (whatever)....."

You: "Hmmm….well, we're coming up with a nickname for you tonight. That's my new mission. Before the night is out, Jenny Elizabeth Henderson is going to be called…….(looking thoughtful).....We. Shall. See. (teasing smile)."

Notice the cliffhanger here. We haven't finalized the conversation about her nickname.

Even better, notice the implication here: you're going to spend the rest of the night together while you figure out what her nickname will be.

She might even start making suggestions about what her nickname should be as the attraction builds.

Be playful in a situation like this. Give her a couple nicknames throughout the night and see which one fits best. Base the name on things you learn about her or things she does during the interaction.

Fooling Around

Let's dispel a myth. Some guys may look at this conversation and think: Pinky swear game? Nicknames? This sounds childish. This would never work on a hot woman.

Pay attention here because this is critical: *Everyone wants to feel like a kid again.*

People (especially women) spend half their waking lives figuring out how to look young. How to feel young. How to be young.

You'd be surprised how many hot babes were ugly ducklings in high school.

The prom queens of the world often end up becoming washed up hags. And it's the girls nobody noticed that come into their primes later in life.

Lots of girls trembled their way through their youth just like lots of guys did. If you can make her feel like a kid again even for a moment (but this time with fun, positive and challenging emotions that let her feel the excitement of youth she never had). If you can whisk her away to some exciting emotional world where she can have carefree fun, she will be entranced by you.

Equally important: **It's not the line**. **It's the man**. It's not what you say. It's *who* is saying it. This should be ingrained in your minds by now. A man who fully embraces the Carefree Man mindset and projects that to the world, can have the conversation above with a 10 and she will be deathly curious about him.

Where Name Assumptions Work Best

As I've said, not everything works in every scenario. In some cases, guessing her name won't fit the circumstances.

I find this works best when you and her "just notice each other."

For example, you turn in your chair at the coffee shop and she's right there. Your eyes meet. And you say inquisitively: "You're name is Amber isn't it."

Or you walk up to the bar. You make eye contact with the cute bartender, you look inquisitive and say: "Your name is Amber isn't it?"

These are examples of you two "just noticing each other."

Where this doesn't seem as natural is, for example: You see a girl from a distance. During the day or in a bar. You maybe even check each other out a few times.

Then you walk toward her, and she sees you coming.

In this case, you're not "just noticing each other."

So it seems less spontaneous to walk 20 feet across a room, while she sees you coming, and then to say: "Hi, your name is Amber isn't it."

(But again, it's the man. A carefree man can make almost anything work).

So if the circumstances don't seem right, here's you fallback line:

"Hi, I'm [whatever]. Who are you?"

This is different from "what's your name?" And different is good.

Where Are You From Assumptions

Let's move on to the next common starter topic: Where are you from?

You're going to see all the same conversation techniques here: assumptions, cliffhangers and changing the subject.

You can start this conversation thread with a general assumption. Or an assumption based on information you know about her already. For example:

"Well with a nickname like Peaches….you gotta be from Georgia." (something that is plausible, but probably wrong).

"Well with a nickname like Peaches…...you gotta be from Alaska." (something that doesn't make sense, and is clearly wrong).

Or, if you had just used the fallback name opener: "Hi, I'm [whatever]. Who are you?" and you don't know anything about her:

"You look like a Texas girl to me."
"You seem like you're from Italy."
"You're a Cali girl aren't you?"

Let's compare this to name assumptions.

With name assumptions, it's easy to be wrong, because there are millions of names.
Remember: wrong is what you want. You want her to wonder why you think that.

With *where are you from* assumptions, it's a lot easier to be right. And you don't want to be right. That's boring.

For example, if you're hitting on a girl in LA and you're like: You're a Cali girl aren't you?

She's like: "yeah…….. (like fucking duh!)"

Obviously that would be stupid and pointless.

So make sure that when you guess, you guess wrong.

Where Are You From Example 1

Let's start with the Peaches scenario follow up:

You: "Well with a nickname like Peaches…...you gotta be from Alaska."
Her: "What? What does peaches have to do with Alaska?"
You: "Peaches are a cold weather fruit."
Her: "No they're not."
You: "You clearly know nothing about peaches."
Her: "*YOU* clearly know nothing about peaches. Peaches are usually grown in the south, like Georgia and South Carolina."
You: "So is that where you're from then? Georgia or South Carolina?"
Her: "What do you think based on my accent?"

You: "Hmmm…..I"m not sure. Tell me why your mom called you peaches and then I'll guess."
Her: (and now is an opportunity for her to tell you story)

Breakdown:

- You're playing on (and using) the nickname.
- You're guessing something wrong (and not logical - bonus!), which spurs curiosity and conversation.
- You say things she disagrees with (not logical stuff) to spark intrigue.
- You change the subject so disagreeing doesn't turn into arguing (because arguing is pointless).
- She tells you guess, and you don't do it (you defer it) thus showing her that you're in control of this conversation and you don't just do what she says.
- You leave a cliffhanger that you will guess where she's from later.
- You transition so now she's telling you a story.
- You're non-linear by going "backward" from 'where she's from', to the origin of the nickname.

Now, what if the assumption was more generic, like:

"You look like a Texas girl to me."
"You seem like you're from Italy."

"You're a Cali girl aren't you."

Then, when she asks what makes you think that, you're response is very similar to earlier:

"I don't know (curious smirk)…...you just look like a Cali to me."
"I'm not sure (curious smirk)…...you're just giving me that Texas vibe."
"I'm not sure (curious smirk)….…there's just something about you. You must at least be of Italian descent."

Notice that "you must at least be of Italian descent" is another assumption.

This is the opposite of asking the boring: "so are you of Italian descent?" to which she would probably say "no" and then you're stuck dealing with her boring answer."

Baby Step to Descent

Where are you from usually means "where were you born and raised." From there, an easy baby-step topic change is to go to family descent.

It can also sometimes can create a small emotional connection if there is something you can both relate to (like if she's half Russian and half Cherokee and you're half Russian and half Jamaican, then you have the Russian half in common - you can both relate to a Russian parent, perhaps).

It can also provide great information when you're trying to determine her nickname. For example if she's of British descent, you might caller Fish-n-Chips or Sassy Little Tart or Austin Powers.

Hopefully this goes without saying, but don't call her anything offensive if there's a derogatory nickname in the vernacular for people of that descent.

Where Are You From Example 2

Let's do a full example:

You: "Hi, I'm Dylan. Who are you?"
Her: "Tara."
(the hands shake)
You: "You seem like you're from Minnesota." [ASSUMPTION]
Her: "Why do you think that?"
You: "I don't know……..say '*Cheese Curds*' for me and let me hear your accent." [DEFERRING YOUR ANSWER / TELLING HER WHAT TO DO]
Her: "Cheese Curds."
You: "Yep (nodding to yourself in confirmation). Definitely Minnesota through and through." [CONTINUING NON-LOGICAL REASONING]
Her: "I'm from New Jersey."

You: "Oohww……(looking playfully disappointed)
[TEASING HER]
Her: "What?"
You: "I have a love / hate relationship with Jersey
girls. [MILD PUSH - LIKE PERHAPS YOU HAD A
BAD EXPERIENCE WITH JERSEY GIRLS OR
SOMETHING]
Her: "Oh really? Why?"
You: "It's complicated. Guess where I'm from?" [NOT
ANSWERING THE QUESTION / CHANGING THE
SUBJECT]
Her: "Say 'Cheese Curds.'"
You: "I'm not from Minnesota." [PLAYING ALONG,
BUT NOT DOING SPECIFICALLY WHAT SHE
SAYS]
Her: "I'm gonna guess……...Florida."
You: "(acting like that's the dumbest guess ever -
palm to forehead, shaking head, etc.) Seriously…...do
I look like I hunt gators in one of those boats with the
huge fans on the back?" [TEASING HER.
PLAYFULLY ACTING LIKE SHE'S CLUELESS]
Her: "So where are you from then?"
You: "(snaps fingers in an "ah ha" moment) It just
dawned on me, you're middle name is Valentina isn't
it?" [DEFERRING YOUR ANSWER / CHANGING
THE SUBJECT / ASSUMING HER NAME --
remember in this example we hadn't assumed
anything about names at the beginning]
Her: "(laughs) Valentina?"
You: "Yeah don't all Jersey girls have the middle
name Valentina? [NON-LOGICAL STATEMENT]

Her: "(lol) I don't know what you're talking about."
You: "What's your middle name then Tara from the Jersey Shore. [ASSUMING SHE'S FROM THE SHORE, WHEN SHE NEVER SAID THAT]
Her: "I didn't say I was from the Shore."
You: "Well where are you from then Tara Valentina?" [REITERATING THE MIDDLE NAME ASSUMPTION]
Her: "It's Kendra. Tara Kendra Larson from Cherry Hill New Jersey."
You: "Well good to know you Tara Kendra Larson from Cherry Hill New Jersey.
(shake hands again - getting to the last name is like meeting again -- never sacrifice a chance to touch).
You: "Tara Kendra huh? Was your nickname '*TK*' when you were kid?" [JUST KEEP GOING...LET THE CLIFFHANGERS FROM BEFORE HANG OUT THERE UNTIL THEY NATURALLY COME BACK UP].
Her: "You haven't told me your middle and last name."
You: "My last name is Laughlin. But you have to guess my middle name." [PARTIALLY ANSWERING (because remember if all you do is defer and not answer then you're just a dick) AND GIVING HER AN INSTRUCTION TO GUESS.]
Her: "I'll guess your middle name, but only if you tell me why you have a love / hate with girls from Jersey first. And don't say "it's complicated.""
You: "So I dated this Jersey girl a while back. She was hot and sassy. Kind of like you (wink). But she did this thing.....Ahh I just couldn't stand it."
[SHOWING PRESELECTION / PARTIALLY

ANSWERING THE QUESTION, BUT DROPPING
ANOTHER CLIFFHANGER].

Her: "What?"

You: "I can't say." [TEASING / DELAYING]

Her: "Tell me or I'm not guessing your middle name."

You: "Alright I'll tell you. But you have to guess my middle name *and* tell me the origin of Larson. That's Scandinavian right?" [AGAIN, YOU CAN'T JUST DELAY. BUT YOU CAN ALWAYS THROW IN CONDITIONS TO SHOW YOU'RE IN CHARGE OF THE CONVERSATION]

Her: "Tell me what she did."

You: "Do we have a deal?" [MAKING SURE SHE'S AGREEING AND NOT JUST TELLING YOU WHAT TO DO]

Her: "Deal."

You: (with fun, playful animation and drama) "OK…..oh this is bad…...ok she used to love fresh squeezed lemonade. She'd buy these big bags of lemons at Costco. But her hands would get tired, so she'd put the lemons on the countertop, and then……. sit on them. Then she'd squeegee all the juice into a pitcher. It was disgusting. And the countertop was all sticky all the time." [TELLING A COMPLETELY ILLOGICAL STORY / BEING OVERLY DRAMATIC]

Her: (hopefully laughing) "That's bullshit!"

You: "Swear………(pausing, looking at her seriously while she recovers laughing) Oh my god, you do that too don't you? It's a Jersey thing isn't it? Oh My God that's it, I'm not attracted to you (say that playfully /

with a smirk). [CONTINUING THE ILLOGICAL STORY AND THEN TURNING IT ONTO HER / PUSH HER WITH THE DISQUALIFIER: I'M NOT ATTRACTED TO YOU]

Her: "I do not squeeze lemons with my ass. You are so full of shit."

You: "So what's my middle name?" [CHANGING THE SUBJECT / GOING BACK TO AN OPEN LOOP]

Her: "Probably *full of shit* is your middle name."

You: "Wrong. Try again."

Her: "(thinking).....Pinocchio."

You: "You are not good at this game.....which means.......you must be Polish. Is Larson a Polish name." [CHANGING THE SUBJECT]

Her: "Norwegian. My grandparents live in Norway."

You: "How many times have you been over there?

Her: "As a kid we used to go every summer. But it's been a while."

You: "If I went to Norway, what would you recommend I do while I'm there?"

And now you can transition into her talking about her experiences as a kid in Norway, what she liked over there, what her grandparents do (or did) for a living. Whatever. A slightly more in-depth, personal conversation which starts the transition into Phase 3 of the Attraction Steps.

In addition, there are still some unclosed loops hanging out there from that conversation (like why you assumed she was from the Shore). You can always return to any of those later on. For example, she does something Snooki-ish, you can ask: "You sure you're from Cherry Hill? That was an awfully Shore-ish move."

Also, she still has to guess your middle name. So return to that later on with a subject change like: "Wait a minute, you still haven't guessed my middle name."

Remember that you don't have to go in any particular order. Start with an assumption about something, and just go from there. Leave cliffhangers and return to them later.

Compare that conversation to:

You: "Hi, I'm Dylan. What's your name?"
Her: "Tara."
You: "Where are you from?"
Her: "New Jersey."
You: "What's your middle name?
Her: "Kendra. What's yours?
You: "Paul."
You: "So um...are you of European descent?"

You see the difference. This second conversation is stiff, boring and even uncomfortable. It doesn't spark curiosity. It's just bland. It shows why lots of guys have so much trouble keeping conversations going.

Lighthearted Disqualifiers

Disqualifiers are another great technique to sprinkle in. Remember this is one tool in the arsenal. You don't need to use it all the time.

Disqualifiers are "pushes." Remember that everything in attraction is giving and taking away. Pushing and pulling.

You generally don't want to start with a disqualifier. Hold off for at least a minute or two. Better yet, hold off until you feel some curiosity from her. If a girl has no curiosity about you and you drop "too bad I'm not attracted to you." She'll just be like "great, piss off then."

Disqualifiers should be delivered playfully, as a joke. Have a smirk on your face. They need to be lighthearted. My favorite disqualifiers are:

- I can tell we're not going to get along
- It's too bad I'm not attracted to you (then later: that's it, I'm definitely not attracted to you)
- It's too bad we're not attracted to each other (for a bit later in the conversation)
- You're such a nice girl, you shouldn't be hanging around a guy like me
- You're such a nice girl, we really need to find you a nice boyfriend

The first one is the simplest. You can drop this randomly (remember not too often) whenever she says pretty much anything.

Her: "Yeah me and my family are big Trojans fans."
You: "That's it. I can tell we're not going to get along."

Her: "Yeah I only eat tofu cheeseburgers."
You: "That's it. I can tell we're not going to get along."

The next one is great if she says something where your initial reaction might be "that's really [something positive]." For example:

You: "That's really cute. It's too bad I'm not attracted to you."
You: "That's really funny. It's too bad I'm not attracted to you."
You: "That's really sexy. It's too bad I'm not attracted to you."

This is a pull/push combo. You pull her in with "that's really [something positive]." And then you push her away with "Too bad I'm not attracted to you."

The next one is great (generally a little further into the conversation) when you both agree on something. Particularly like a "wow we agree" moment.

For example: She says something that you totally agree with.

You say: "That is totally how I see it. Wow we would make the perfect couple. It's too bad we're not attracted to each other."

Basically drop it at a time where you can start off with: "wow we would make the cutest couple, or the sexiest couple, or the funniest couple, etc."

The last two you can use anytime she says something sweet or innocent.

Her: "And then this baby chipmunk came running across the grass and jumped right onto the lounge chair."
You: "Wow…...you're such a nice girl, you shouldn't be hanging around a guy like me."

Remember everything is said as a playful joke. Then just change the subject.

Your Surroundings

You can use anything in your surroundings to change the subject. If you see anything you're curious about, just randomly change the subject to that. For example:

Her: "Probably *full of shit* is your middle name."
You: "Hey look at that (you point to an 1800s spitoon the bar is using as a tip jar)."

Her: "What?"
You: "Is that a spitoon?"
Her: "I have no idea."
You: "It is. It looks authentic too. So honest opinion, do you think they should bring back the spitoon?"
Her: "That's gross. A bunch of guys spitting their cigar mouths into the same bucket.
You: "It's a spitoon, not a bucket."
Her: "Whatever."
You: "So anyway, about the lemons. I'm not kidding, she used to squeeze the juice by sitting on them."

So literally anything even remotely interesting in your surroundings can be used to quickly change the subject. Particularly useful at a heated moment when she's calling you full of shit, for example. Just change the subject. Change, change and change again. She will find it attractive as hell.

Also, I brought the conversation back to the lemons quickly above, just to keep the example short. No need to. Drag the spittoon thing out as long as it remains interesting. And if that leads to a new conversational thread, unrelated to the lemons, change the subject to that.

You can come back to the lemons sometime later, or not at all. Just keep moving forward in the conversation and let things come back up naturally.

What Do You Do For Fun Example

You: "Hey, I'm Logan. Who are you?"
Her: "Kacee."
(the hands shake)
You: "You know…..you seem like a yoga chick to me." [ASSUMPTION]
Her: "Why makes you think that?"
You: "I don't know……..you seem like some of the girls in my yoga class." [DEFERRING ANSWER / SAYING SOMETHING TO SPARK CURIOSITY]
Her: "You're in a yoga class?"
You: "What, you don't believe me?" [NOT ANSWERING]
Her: "(playfully) Let me see you do a pose."
You: "Is that your best pick up line? You must be from LA." [ACTING LIKE SHE'S HITTING ON YOU / CHANGING THE SUBJECT / ASSUMPTION]
Her: "Why?"
You: "Because LA girls are forward like that. Knowing a guy for 15 seconds and asking him to pose naked." [ILLOGICAL ANSWER]
Her: "Lol I did not say pose naked. I said give me your best downward dog."
You: "Seriously, if you want to check out my butt you can just ask."   [CONTINUING TO ACT LIKE SHE'S HITTING ON YOU]
Her: "I *do not* want to check out your butt."
You: "So are you a yoga chick from LA or what? Let's see your downward California dog.

[CHANGING SUBJECT BACK TO OPEN
CLIFFHANGERS]
Her: "Why, you want to check out my butt?"
You: "That was not an original line. (playful smirk /
wink)" [TEASING].
Her: "Yeah I've been doing yoga for 6 years. Yoga
and pilates. I'm also vegan."
You: "That's it. I can tell we're not going to get
along." [DISQUALIFIER].
Her: "Why, you predigest against vegans?"
You: "Of course not. But I can't date anyone who's
been doing yoga less than 7 years." [POSSIBLY
LOGICAL ANSWER WHICH TURNS OUT TO BE
RIDICULOUS].
Her: "Oh really.....how long have you been doing it?
You: "Last Tuesday was my first class."
Her: "(laughing) I see. So that's why you won't show
me your downward dog."
You: "Yeah....on Tuesday the instructor told me that
my downward dog looked more like a dead dog, then
she kicked me out of the class. [ILLOGICAL
ANSWER]
Her: "(laughs). I believe the first part. But I doubt the
instructor kicked you out.
You: "You'd be surprised.....that instructor was a little
fiesty. I think she was a vegan from LA."
[CONTINUING ILLOGICAL / GOING BACK TO
VEGAN AND LA]
Her: "I'm not from LA."
You: "Do tell."
Her: "You've never heard of where I'm from."

You: "I've heard of the world. Wait a second (playfully nervous)……..are you from somewhere else….[ILLOGICAL ANSWER]

Her: "I'm from Sullivan Illinois"

You: "(Palm of hand against forehead / looking at her like she's pitiful) Where?" [ACTING LIKE THAT WAS THE DUMBEST ANSWER IN THE WORLD]

Her: "I told you you've never heard of it.

You: "Do they have running water there?" [PLAYING UP THE SMALL TOWN STEREOTYPE]

Her: "Where are you from?"

You: "Hold on now, we have to get to the bottom of this. What is your last name? I need to Google Sullivan Illinois and see if everyone has this same last name. [NOT ANSWERING QUESTION / CONTINUING STEREOTYPE]

Her: "Tell me where you're from first Mister Dead Dog. And then I'll tell you my last name."

You: "I'll give you one guess. And it's not Sullivan Illinois." [NOT DOING WHAT SHE SAYS / GIVING HER THE TASK TO GUESS]

Her: "New York."

You: "Close. I'm from Pittsburgh Pennsylvania, Misses Kacee Something from Sullivan Illinois. [GOING BACK TO THE LAST NAME W/O DIRECTLY ASKING FOR IT]

Her: "Jackson. Kacee Jackson."

You: "Good to know you Kacee Jackson. I'm Logan Foster."

(shake hands -- hold for a slightly longer embrace at this point)

Her: "So what do you do for fun Logan Foster?"

With her starting to ask you questions, you've reached curiosity and are starting to move towards Phase 6.

Stacking Assumptions

Let's take a look at this line from the previous conversation:

You: "Is that your best pick up line? You must be from LA." [ACTING LIKE SHE'S HITTING ON YOU / CHANGING THE SUBJECT / ASSUMPTION]

The key thing to notice is the assumption "you must be from LA." Not long before this, you made the assumption that she was a yoga chick. That is still an open conversational thread. She hasn't given you any indication if she's a yoga chick or not at this point.

That shouldn't stop you from making another assumption if flows naturally with the conversation.

We said earlier that if all you do is make assumptions, then you seem like a dick. That's true. But that shouldn't stop you from "stacking" a few assumptions one after the other if the situation allows it flow naturally.

Stack a few, and then the conversation will flow back to each one in due time.

Acting Like She's Hitting On You

Let's look at this sentence again. This one accomplished a lot for us.

You: "Is that your best pick up line? You must be from LA." [ACTING LIKE SHE'S HITTING ON YOU / CHANGING THE SUBJECT / ASSUMPTION]

Acting like a girl is hitting on you is a great way to tease. You can sprinkle these in whenever you want. Here's a few good ones:

- Is that your best pick up line?
- Stop trying to hit on me, I'm not that easy.
- You can tell me fun stories about your (dad, mom, brother, grandmother, etc), but I'm not ready to meet them yet. I only met you 5 minutes ago (or a week ago, or whatever the case may be).
- Stop looking at me like that. It's making me uncomfortable.

The first two can be used anytime she says something that could be interpreted as a pick up line (even if it's a stretch). Like:

Her: "Wow, I love your shoes. My brother has a pair just like them."
You: "Wow, is that your best pick up line?"

Her: "That's really sweet that you volunteer at the puppy shelter on Saturdays."
You: "Hey… stop trying to hit on me, I'm not that easy."

The next one you can drop anytime she finishes telling a story about her family.

The last one you can drop usually when she's laughing hard and/or looking at you with "those eyes."

As always, fun, playful, tone. Smirk.

Signs She is Curious About You

The conversations above are examples of how to make her curious about you.

Building curiosity should not take long. Anywhere from 1 to 10 minutes; but let's say 5 minutes as a general rule of thumb.

Here is the key takeaway: if you practice and master the techniques above, so you can have fun, challenging conversations that spark curiosity, you only need to cover some combination of these topics:

names, nicknames, where you're both from, descent, what both people do for fun, surroundings.

You may also drop in a playful disqualifier here or there.

You don't need to make it more complicated than that.

You don't need to cover an encyclopedia of topics.

Remember you have about 5 minutes, so there is no

need cover more topics at this point → as long as you

can create a fun, challenging conversation using

these topics.

Important: remember that it's the fun, challenging *WAY* that you interact that makes her curious. It's not the topics.

It's the man. Not the specifics of what the man is talking about.

The reason why lots of guys get stuck in awkward silences and (a) never know what to say and (b) think that they need to be prepared with pages and pages of smalltalk topics, is because the *WAY* they discuss the topics above is boring, and because it's boring it goes by way too fast.

For example, if a guy just does a question and answer session about the topics above, he could cover everything above in 30 seconds. Then he'd be standing there in awkwardness wondering what to say next.

So change the way you make small talk by mastering the techniques above. At the beginning it may feel uncomfortable to talk like that. Uncomfortable is good. It's what we want. There's a land filled with beautiful women on the other side of discomfort.

And it's only uncomfortable because your current speech patterns are just not used to it. So pick one technique at a time and practice it. In the Action Steps included in the Daytime and Nighttime supplements, you will see many of these techniques specifically assigned for practice.

Finally remember that curiosity about you should be established in about 5 minutes. If you've been talking with her for 10 minutes or more and she doesn't appear interested in you, it's time to move on. This happens. Remember that every guy who appears to attract women with ease has 10x the number of rejections under his belt as compared to successes. So if it seems to be going nowhere after 10 minutes, thank her for the great conversation and move on.

Now if you're doing things right and she's becoming curious about you, these are the signs you will see:

- She starts asking you questions.
- She re-initiates the conversation if you've paused.
- She playfully hits you in the shoulder.
- She's laughing.
- She's smiling.
- She's playing with her hair.
- She's shifted her body so her shoulders and waist are facing you.
- Her feet are pointing at you.
- She's looking at you just a little too long before looking away.
- She'll move locations if you suggest it.
- She does what you say when you counter her test (see more on tests later).
- She is engaged in the conversation you're both having.

You should see a couple of these signs, but you don't need to see them all. It should be pretty obvious whether she's enjoying talking to you or not, so don't over-complicate what you 'need to see' before moving on to the next phase.

Here's an extremely important takeaway about transitioning from Phase 2: Curiosity to Phase 3: Fascination, which should put your mind at ease: you have a lot of wiggle room here.

There is no precise moment. There's no distinct line that says: *leaving Phase 2 and entering Phase 3.* This is because you can (and should) transition back and forth between low investment banter (Phase 2 small talk) and high investment conversation (Phase 3 deeper conversations -- to be discussed shortly) during the transition.

In fact, not only during the transition, but all the time. Because low investment banter (Phase 2) is the lightest, most playful form of conversation, and should be mixed into all deeper conversations that happen later in the process.

In other words, you never completely stop Phase 2 low investment banter. Because you never stop, there is no exact transition time, and should make things feel much more smooth and natural.

In the next chapter, we'll discuss how to interject Phase 2 low investment banter in between deeper conversations.

Storm The Beach - How To Walk Into A Bar

Before moving on to deeper, high investment conversations, let's look at the best way to walk into a bar and make a party for yourself or your group.

You can do this alone. Or if your wings are doing this too, then you guys can really cover a lot of ground quickly.

When you walk into a bar or club, you're going to Storm the Beach.

What does storming the beach mean in a military context? It means you charge forward blowing up everything in sight. You blast the first thing in front of you. Then you blast the next thing. And the next thing. You swarm. You hit everything in sight.

That's what we're going to do. Except instead of actual explosives, we're going to hit women with IEADs.

IEADs - Improvised Explosive Attraction Devices

This may sound complicated, but it's really quite simple.

Storming The Beach and Dropping IEADs means simply this: You're going to walk through the door and start talking to every girl that is in your path. The purpose of this is to (1) start talking and hitting on women immediately because it only gets harder the longer you wait and (2) to establish preselection all over the place. More on these points after the examples.

The moment you walk through the door, look around. The first girl you see, you walk up to her. It doesn't matter what she looks like. You're not trying to bag this one. You just need to start talking and establishing preselection. So just do it. No thinking. No hesitation.

Walk up to her like you own the fucking bar. Stick out your hand. Have a huge smile on your face and say:

"Hi, I'm Caleb. I'm shy."

That will make her laugh.

Then you immediately go into an assumption. Your intention is to meet, drop an assumption, get one piece of information from her, and leave with an open cliffhanger behind you. Here' we go:

You walk in. The first one is a fugly who's just walking by.

You: "Hi, I'm Mason. I'm shy."
Her: "(laughing, shaking your hand) You don't look shy."
You: "You seem like you're of German descent."
Her: "Really? Why do you say that?"
You: "I'm not sure (looking at her skeptically)....there's just something about you. Say Dusseldorf. Actually, say it 3 times, quickly."

Her: "Dusseldorf. Dussleford. Duselddfse."

You: "(looking at her like she's a complete idiot / shaking your head) Nope...definitely not of German descent. And (looking confused), who are you, by the way?"

Her: "I'm Kelsey."

You: "Good to know you Kelsey (maybe the hands shake again). I'm gonna get a drink, I'll see you around."

Then start walking.

The next one is a hottie at a hightop table.

You: "Hi, I'm Mason. I'm shy."

Her: "(laughing, shaking your hand) Hi. I'm Sophie.

You: "Good to know you Sophie. Sophie, that's French right?"

Her: "Swiss. I was named after Grandmother."

You: "Huh. You know, you seem like an East Coast girl to me."

Her: "Nope. Born and raised right here in Sacramento.

You: "Not exactly a world traveler are you?"

Her: "I've traveled!"

You: "Name 3 places you've traveled."

Her: "Canada."

You: "(interrupting) That's not really traveling."

Her: "Ahem... I've also been to Australia and New Zealand."

You: "Not bad. Well my little Swiss chocolate traveler, I'm gonna grab a drink. I'll see you around."

Next there are two cute girls at a table right near the bar. The seem to have been watching you talk to Sophie (hopefully - because this is what we want for preselection purposes).

You walk up to the table and stick your hand out to the hotter one.

You: "Hi, I'm Mason. I'm shy."
Her: "I see how shy you've been hitting on two girls already since you walked in."
You: "What are you a detective?"
Her: "Just observant, that's all."
You: "(ignoring that) So if you're Sherlock (looking inquisitively at the hot one). You must be Watson (turning to the less hot one and sticking out your hand)."
Her: "I'm Sabrina. (hands shake)"
You: "Good to know you Sabrina. Hey (pretending to half-whisper) what's your friend's name? She's kinda looking at me all googly-eyes….and it's making me a little nervous."
Sabrina: "(giggling) Her name is Vickey. And she's *not* looking at you all googly-eyes.
You: "(looking back at Vickey with a confident smirk and seductive eye contact, but saying nothing -- trust me, if she wasn't looking at you with googly-eyes before, she is now -- pause for 1 beat too long, then).

Alright my little detectives, I'm gonna grab a drink while you too keep casing the scene. (allow your eye contact to slowly fade off of Vicky's...and walk)."

Now you're at the bar.

Breakdown.

So there's a couple of great things you've done here.

First. Talking to girls in a bar is always harder the longer you wait. Therefore you should always start the instant you walk in. Make it a habit. Talk to any chick you can find right away. It doesn't matter what she looks like. It doesn't matter what you say. Just start talking.

Second. By talking to multiple girls in a row in rapid fashion, you've made sure that women see you talking to and laughing with other women. Don't make the mistake of thinking that if a woman (let's say the hottie you actually want) sees you talking to other women, that hottie will lose interest. It's the exact opposite.

The more you talk to women, the more other woman will want you. That's called preselection. This is what you want. By talking to multiple women in a row, you will have preselection-IEADs blowing up everywhere.

Make it a habit to talk to at least 3 women before you even order a drink.

Later it will be easy to go back and talk to all those women again. Really, it's so simple and natural to initiate conversation with someone that you've spoken to already -- even if it was just for a minute.

Once you get a drink, you should continue Storming The Beach. Try to talk to between 5 and 10 women as soon as possible. This will get the night started off right and the bar will become your personal playground.

Remember, all your doing is introducing yourself, making an assumption, collecting one piece of information, and getting out. That's it.

What To Tell The Fugly One

This is an optional technique you can test out for yourself as you get comfortable.

What you do here is you tell the fugly one that she's hot. Or looks good. Or whatever.

Remember that different is attractive. The fugly one doesn't get told that she's hot, or looks good, that often. So it's definitely different.

If you tell her that, she will be head-over-heels for you.

Now you might be asking, why would I want that?

Well, as you probably know, women generally go to bars together. They travel in packs. So if a fugly one is walking past, like in the example above, most likely her friends are somewhere nearby.

Preselection means that you've been preselected by *a female*. It doesn't matter if she's fugly or hot.

So, if the fugly one is there with 4 hot girlfriends, and you've just dropped this line on her, rest assured she'll be back with her girlfriends raving about some hot stud she just talked to. She'll literally be drooling about you.

Then all 4 of the hot friends will *have to* check you out. When they do, you know what they'll see? You talking to other women elsewhere in the bar as you Storm the Beach.

Now you have 4 hot women that just got hit with a preselection-IEAD from afar (seeing you talk to other women) and with a second preselection-IEAD from someone they know (their fugly friend raving about you). This will make that group of 5 really simple to approach later on. In fact, they will be waiting anxiously for you to come over there.

The reason I say this technique is optional is because sometimes the fugly one can be extremely interested and aggressive at regaining your attention. So just be aware.

Here's how you would drop the line:

You: "(looking at her like she's a complete idiot / shaking your head) Nope...definitely not of German descent. And (looking confused), who are you, by the way?
Her: "I'm Kelsey."
You: "Good to know you Kelsey (maybe the hands shake again). I'm gonna get a drink, I'll see you around. By the way, you're looking sexy as hell. (then walk)"

Simple.

What To Tell The Hot One

You already know this. Everything we've gone over about conversation in this chapter *is* what you tell the hot one.

But just so there's no confusion with the last section:

You tell the fugly one: that she's hot
You tell the hot one: that you're not attracted to her

Remember, the opposite of what is expected is different, and different is attractive.

Just to be completely clear: you can tell the fugly one that she's hot right away.

However, you DO NOT tell the hot one that you're not attracted to her right away. You wait until some level of attraction has been established. She needs to be curious about you already. So hold off on the "it's too bad I'm not attracted to you" playful disqualifier until you see some of the signs above about her being curious about you (like laughing, turning toward you, playing with her hair, etc).

How To Handle Tests In a Bar

Guys often ask me how to handle a girls tests. These are often called shit tests. I'm going to give you word for word, the best way to handle the most common shit test you will ever hear in a bar. Specifically: "buy me a drink."

But before we get there, let's clarify a few things.

Remember that the underlying goal of this entire training is to transform *you* into the highest version of yourself. The version that women find irresistable. Now is a good time to remind ourselves of that because we just went through pages and pages of "lines" that will help you get started making free-flowing, endless conversation with women.

Practicing lines and techniques is perfectly acceptable at the beginning. You need a place to start. Just don't forget that "lines" is not the point. The point is *you*. When you are the highest version of yourself, what you say doesn't matter.

With that in mind, why do you think guys get so many shit tests? To answer that, let's compare everything we just went through about Storming The Beach, to this:

This is how most guys enter a bar:

They walk in. They start scoping it out. They start looking for a table. The start looking for a cocktail waitress. The start looking to order a drink. They start looking around to see who's in the venue. They start looking around to see what kind of hot chicks are around. They start sipping their drink. They start talking amongst themselves in the group. If there's TVs, maybe they glance at them. They watch people on the dance floor. They drink a little more and maybe start preparing themselves to approach some women. The wallflowers of the group are probably getting ready for a long night of standing there, and standing there, and standing there, forever.....and maybe, eventually, when they're liquored up enough, some of them, might, approach a woman.

How does that compare to what we went through above?

What you should be noticing is that by the time most guys finally get around to approaching a woman, all the women in the venue have seen him standing around. Shifting from foot to foot. Nursing his beer. Maybe slamming a couple drinks to get lubed up for the approach. Talking to his friends. Whatever.

They know he's nervous. They know he's not the highest version of himself. So they shit test the hell out of him if he ever does approach.

On the other hand, when women see you Storming the Beach and talking Woman 1. Then Woman 2. Then Women 5 through 10 (and don't forget the fugly one who went drooling back to her crew about the stud she just talked to). When they see you doing that, and then maybe, if she's lucky, you finally arrive to talk to her, do you think she's going to test you?

Anything's possible, but most likely not. She's way too curious for that. You're Beach Storming approach is so different from every other guy standing around nursing beers, that she is really curious to talk to you.

She's interested in the guy who all the other women were laughing with. So she's not going to ask anything which might make *you* lose interest in talking to *her*. Anything that might make you ditch her and go back to the other 5 women you were just talking to moments earlier.

The point is, when you become the highest version of yourself and you start dealing with women the way this course has taught you, the amount of times you encounter tests will be greatly reduced.

With that said, nobody's perfect. So here's my #1 way to deal with the most common test of them all: "Buy me a drink."

Generally there are two acceptable ways to deal with this test. You either (1) don't agree to buy the drink, or you (2) agree to buy the drink, but add conditions to the arrangement.

I'm going to talk primarily about number (2) because I have the absolute silver bullet conditions to share with you (which work every time).

Before we get into that, let me address number (1) briefly. Obviously you can't just say "no." That probably won't get you anywhere. So usually this is either combined with something that turns it around on her. Like: "how about you buy me the first drink, and I'll buy the next round of drinks."

That's saying no, but still sort of adding conditions.

You can also be more aggressive and be like: "I think I'll pass. But if you want to grab another round, feel free to grab me one as well."

All of this can work. Remember, anything can work. It's the man. Not the line.

But in general, these are more aggressive and you're more likely to lose the girl. So just be aware of that if you want to try these out.

Now, here's what I recommend instead.

Regardless of if you do (1) or (2), you always start off being non-reactive.

I hear a lot of confusion about what being non-reactive means. So let's clarify.

Non-reactive essentially means having a delayed reaction. You start off by having no reaction at all (i.e. literally standing there with no change of body position, facial expression, or anything else) for a short time. Then you react.

I recommend 4 seconds. A solid 4 seconds. Don't rush it. Here's how it works.

You hear the words: "buy me a drink."

At that moment, you become frozen in place. If you're looking and smiling at her, you keep looking and smiling at her. If you're looking someplace else. You keep looking someplace else. Your body doesn't move. Your head doesn't move. You're eyes don't move. Your facial expression doesn't change.

You just freeze, in place, and count
1….....2……..3…….4.

What does this do?

Well the first thing is that's it's different. The common response would be to agree or disagree with the drink request immediately (i.e. to have an immediate reaction).

Second, because you're not moving or showing any change in expression, there is no way for her to 'read' what you're thinking. That's confusing (which is good because confusing is challenging). It also demonstrates that you are the dominant player in the interaction (i.e. when she tests to get a reaction out of you, she can't get one.)

Third, the 4 seconds (combined with the no change in facial expression / body position) is just long enough for her to wonder if she said something wrong. Or something that would make you walk away.

So you always start with that. And relish the 4 seconds. Don't rush them. She will wait for a reaction. Play around. Make her wait.

My #1 Silver Bullet Conditions

Here are the perfect conditions to add. Just copy this. It works every time.

So, after the 4 seconds of being non-reactive is up, you say: "ok, I'll buy you a drink, but only if you do something first."

She will always ask: "what?"

You say (this is you explaining to her - and you should be animated and demonstrate with your hands/body):

'*You need to stand up and face me. Then you need to stand nice and tall like a soldier standing in formation. Then you need to put your hand up next to your forehead in a military salute*.' (again, you can be demonstrating all this to her)

'*Then you need to say in a clear, loud voice*:'

 "General [Your Name]. This is Lieutenant [Her Name] reporting in for chug, glug and slam duty general sir."

'And you have to say it just like that, otherwise it doesn't count. Then you need to stand there at full attention, with your salute up, until I salute you back.'

(note: in the first part, if she's already standing, just say "turn and face me.")

Giving her these ridiculous conditions is hysterical. And it works wonders. Here's why.

Some women just won't do it (at first). They're too embarrassed (or too sober). So you just change the subject and carry on conversation. But rest assured, the drink issue is coming back, probably quickly. So when she brings it up again. You agree. "Definitely I'll buy you a drink, you just need to do this one teensy weensy little thing first."

Now you've got her stuck between a free drink and acting dumb. Girls who ask for drinks really want free drinks, and they don't necessarily want to act dumb to get them, so she's steamed.

Not at you though, that's the beauty of this. She's steamed at herself. Because you didn't say no. You agreed to what she asked for. You said "yes!" But you added this little caveat that she just can't handle.

The fact that you've got her stuck in this position makes her attraction for you skyrocket.

You have somehow created this power over her that she can't figure out how to get around. So play with it. Relish it. She may try to wheel and deal. Just hold your ground. You will totally buy that drink, but only if…….

Also keep in mind that most women who refuse at first, will come around eventually (and not too long actually because they really want that drink).

For the women that will do it right away, you say the following:

Just as she's standing up, you say: "Now make it convincing, or it doesn't count."

Then play with her and tease her when she can't get it right (not if, when lol).

She will forget the words, or mix them up. When she does make her start over. Be like: "nope." "that wasn't it." "try again." (all playful, obviously).

When she's finally done, and she's standing there with the salute, you start raising your salute hand, very slowly.

Do the 4 second count again. Your hand goes from waist level, up to your forehead in

1…..…..2…..….3……….4 (the suspense will be palpable). Then you salute.

Either way, you have passed the test. Even better, you have given her a test and she's failed (i.e. she did what you told her to do). You literally made her stand up, stand in a goofy position, make a goofy arm gesture, say something ridiculous, and then stand there waiting for you. All to get a vodka tonic. You win. Props.

If she does all that, you've got her hooked. You can move to the next step.

And…..you can buy her a drink too, I suppose.

******

It's time to take action. Go to Daytime Unleashed and complete Action Steps 3 through 7 over the next week or so.

Complete Action Step 3 before going on to Chapter 6.

Complete action Steps 4 through 7 while you go through Chapter 6.

And congratulate yourself. If you've made it this far in the course, a life filled with beautiful women is only weeks away.

Chapter 6: Attraction Phase 3 - Fascination

Before you begin Chapter 6, go to your bonus supplement 7 Mental Exercises to Get You Laid. Read through all of the exercises and select 3 that you think are the most relevant to your personal circumstances. Over the next couple of days, complete the three exercises that you selected.

Conversations That Create An Emotional Connection

Alright this is where the rubber meets the road. Or perhaps where the rubber finds its way between her legs and meets the........well, actually, you're not quite there yet.

First, you're going to fascinate her. To make her think: *wow, is this real?*

When Phase 2 is complete, she's curious about you. She's showing the signs of attraction we mentioned above (at least some of them).

In Phase 3 you will continue to deliver fun, positive and challenging vibes. And you will continue to take them away. This is the same as Phase 2.

The difference now is what you're talking about.

You're now going to transition into deeper conversation and establish an emotional connection with her. Making a emotional connection involves you sharing things about yourself, and her sharing personal things about herself.

Here's the best part. You already know what to share.

If you have completed reading 7 Mental Exercises to Get You Laid, then you already have tons of things to share about yourself. You have more than enough to make any woman fascinated.

So let's put it all together.

There are two ways to have a deeper conversation that establishes an emotional connection:

- Sharing stories

- Asking deeper questions (A deeper question is one that requires her to divulge more personal information. For example, discussing nicknames and what you do for fun, isn't that deep. Asking her if she could change one thing in the world, what would it be? Now that's getting deeper.)

BE CAREFUL: Going deeper does not mean "getting all serious." This is a huge pitfall for guys when trying to transition into deeper topics. If you get all serious, the conversation loses its fun, playful vibe. It becomes boring. It becomes work, like "oh what a pain in the ass that I have to tell this guy all this stuff about me."

So the fun, positive and challenging emotions stays. The pushing, pulling and teasing stays. What happens is that slightly more deeper/serious intervals occur in between.

Let's make this crystal clear.

How The Conversation Changes

In Phase 2 - Curiosity the conversation is basically lite and playful the whole time. In Phase 3 - Fascination, the conversation is lite and playful 50% of the time, with more serious topics/discussion/emotions mixed in the other 50%.

(These 50% breakouts are not set in stone. Don't get hung up on specifics. The point is that mixed into the lite and playful conversation are intervals of deeper/more serious discussion)

This is best demonstrated by example. Here is the same conversation in Phase 2 vs Phase 3 mode.

Let's say you're still in Phase 2 (i.e. you're not completely certain you're seeing the signs of curiosity):

Her: "As a kid we used to go every summer. But it's been a while."
You: "If I went to Norway, what would you recommend I do while I'm there?"
Her: "You definitely need to take one of the ice baths lol."
You: "I know you think I'm hot, but really.....ice bath."
Her: "Psssht. You couldn't handle the ice bath anyway."
You: "How many ice baths have you taken in your life?"
Her: "A lot."
You: "Sounds like you must be an ice queen."
Her: (gives you dirty look)
You: "(putting your hands on both her shoulders to embrace her like she was a pouting child). I'm just kidding Tara Kendra Larson from Cherry Hill New Jersey. I'm sure you're just a lukewarm queen."

Her: (hopefully she elbows you in the ribs)

You: So seriously, how does an ice bath work?

Her: "Well it's not just an ice bath. There's actually a hot bath, like a jacuzzi, and an ice bath right next to it. And you jump from one to the other.

You: "It's supposed to help improve the circulation right?"

Her: "Wait....you know what the ice bath is already?"

You: "I saw a National Geographic once in a dentist's waiting room."

Her: "Well then you definitely need to try it."

You: "I'll keep that in mind. So about downward dog, what tips are you gonna lay on me so………

In this conversation there was basically nothing deep. Just lite conversation mixed with some teasing and then before the topic got stale, you just changed the subject to something else.

There was a lot of great information in here though that you can circle back to later (later in this conversation -- or in any future conversation).

First. You have some new nicknames you can always toss around: Norway; ice queen; ice bath; Scandinavian skinny dipper.

Second. Anything related to jacuzzis, spas, saunas, hot tubs, swimming pools, skinny dipping, showers or baths can have a connection to this story.

Bonus tip - Linking any future conversational thread back to this story helps establish that you two have a shared connection. Here's an example:

You're on a second date. She's at your place for a bottle of wine and a movie. You suggest going down to the jacuzzi:

You: "Hey before we start the movie let's go down to the jacuzzi for 10 minutes and relax the muscles. There's only a hot one sorry to say. No ice bath to cool you down.
Her: "I didn't bring my suit."
You: "That's ok, in Norway they jacuzzi in the buck."
Her: "(smiling) They do not jacuzzi in the buck."
You: "Well little miss unprepared, I'll give you an oversized t-shirt and boxers to wear. You'll look like a miniature Swamp Thing when you climb out dripping wet. But if you're lucky, you'll give me a shoulder massage."
Her: (looking skeptical)
You: "I mean….if you're lucky I'll give you a shoulder massage.
Her: "Ok. That's a deal."

Here's how the same conversation might go in Phase 3 (when we're establishing a deeper connection).

Her: "As a kid we used to go every summer. But it's been a while."

You: "If I went to Norway, what would you recommend I do while I'm there?"

Her: "You definitely need to take one of the ice baths lol."

You: "I know you think I'm hot, but really…..ice bath."

Her: "Psssht. You couldn't handle the ice bath anyway."

You: "So was it your grandparents that took you to your first ice bath?"

Her: "Yeah my grandpa. There was one about a mile from their house. We would go every day about noon. When the 'sun was high in the sky' my grandpa always used to say."

You: "(looking skeptical) Your grandpa said 'when the sun was high in the sky'?"

Her: "Well he said it in Norwegian. But that's what my mom told me it meant."

You: "So were you scared the first time? Like what were the feelings you can remember about going there when you were a kid?"

Her: [Now hopefully she goes into a story about her experiences there. Most memories of childhood are feelings anyway, so prompting the question with "what were the feelings you can remember" should really get her back to those times. This little interval will be more serious as she divulges some personal snippets about herself, her feelings, her past and her family. When she's done…]

You: "You know you can tell me cool stories about your grandpa all day, but I'm not ready to meet him (sly smile / pause while the push sinks in). I'm just messing with you. (pull her in for a quick side-hug) It sounds like you were really lucky to have a great grandfather. So about downward dog.."

The key takeaway is that the conversation is going along nice and playful, just like in Phase 2. But then something is said or asked which prompts a deeper response. And a deeper response will usually take on a deeper, more somber tone.

This is fine for an interval. JUST MAKE SURE TO BRING IT BACK TO LITE AND PLAYFUL AND CHANGE THE SUBJECT.

Percentage Breakdown

Let's clarify the percentages. Again, I don't want you to get hung up on specifics. Just understand the general concept.

In Phase 2: Lite and playful 80% of the time. Perhaps more serious 20%.
In Phase 3: Lite and playful 50% of the time. More serious 50% of the time.

The point is that you are always partially lite and playful, and there can always be some seriousness mixed in. Less seriousness will be mixed in at the beginning and more will be mixed in as you establish a deeper connection.

Storytelling

We've been tackling the problem of "I don't know what to say" pretty hard, but let's not stop yet. Again, this is probably the biggest hang-up guys have. If we can just get past this, everything else will fall into place.

In Phase 2 - Curiosity, we tackled the problem by understanding that you basically should say whatever comes to mind. We established that changing the topic is good. We established that you should make assumptions, leave cliffhangers, use your surroundings, tell her something about yourself, make up nicknames, and other tactics.

In Phase 3 - Fascination, we're going to take it to the next level. You're going to start telling her stories about yourself.

Now if you're concerned like: "wait a minute.....I don't know how to tell stories..." just think about this:

Guys struggling with seduction will go online and rant on and on for hours and hours about: "not knowing what to say."

Wait......did you catch that? They will talk for hours and hours about not knowing what to say......

What is another name for "talking for hours and hours?"

That's right. "Telling a story." Guys will go online and rant out long stories…...about not being able to tell stories……..figure that out….

So, clearly we *all* know how to tell stories. You just need to make one little change.

You need to start telling your stories to women. Particularly hot women you want to sleep with. And stop wasting time telling stories in online forums.

Now let's be clear. Stories doesn't mean dragons and wizards and dumb shit.

It means stories about your life. Stories that will make you a relatable human being.

Stories that will show your emotion. Stories that will allow her to make an emotional connection to you. Stories that will, in turn, cause her to tell you stories back.

It also means stories that demonstrate you're a "high value human being" (more on that coming up).

Telling stories is one of the oldest forms of human communication. People from all cultures have connected with each other through stories for thousands of years.

People have literally lived their entire lives based on information in stories.

Stories are emotional. Women are emotional.

So let's start telling your stories to women.

You have lots of stories to tell already, and you are developing more everyday. Almost every action/activity in this course has a two-fold purpose. The purpose that seems obvious, and the story you get that's related to it.

What To Talk About In Stories

You can tell stories about many things. However there are 7 topics you should focus on. Women cannot help but feel attracted to men who demonstrate these 7 qualities (or at least some of them - you don't have to tell her a story about every one of them).

These are the 7 qualities which demonstrate a "high value human being."

1. You being in a Leadership Role
2. You being a great Communicator
3. You Demonstrating Female Awareness
4. You Demonstrating Fun, Positive and Challenging Emotions

5. You Demonstrating that you're are Improving Yourself Daily
6. You Demonstrating Preselection
7. You Demonstrating High Social Status

Leadership

If you've completed the assignments in 7 Mental Exercises to Change Your Life, you should have a story written down about you in a leadership role.

Any story with you in a leadership position is gold.

Women are subconsciously attracted to leaders. Throughout history leaders are the men who keep the tribe/clan/group safe and in order. Leaders are the men who protect and feed.

Now your story isn't going to be about running tribes and feeding people, but it will still be about leading people in some way.

This can be an official leadership position (like at work or military). Or it can be an unofficial leadership position.

An unofficial leadership position is where you make a decision for a group, and everybody follows, even if you weren't officially the leader.

For example, let's say you're with a group of people at a bar. The bar is closing, but everyone wants the party to keep going. The problem is that no one can decide what to do. This person says this. That person says that. Some girl gets pissed off.

Finally you just announce: "Alright, we're doing [whatever]." Then you go and do it, and everybody follows your lead.

It can also be a story where you were in an official leadership position. You had 3 people working for you, and your boss tells you 1 of them must be let go. It was up to you to decide which one.

Subtle but important point: The point of the story is *not* that you're the leader. The point of the story is something else. It should be a cool story that just happens to demonstrate that you are a leader.

Again, it's not about bragging that you were the leader. It's about sharing an interesting story, and the girl you're talking too sees you as the leader without it ever being stated.

Communication

Great communication is attractive. This can mean verbal, non-verbal (body language) or written communication.

With respect to stories, it can mean (1) a story that demonstrates you in some kind of communication role (like you giving a speech or presentation - where there were great reactions in the audience), or it can simply mean (2) how you are telling a story right now.

If you practice your stories, you will become great at telling them. You will know when to change your voice from high to low. You will know when to pause for dramatic effect. You will know when to be animated and when to be reserved. All of these things will make your story fascinating. And it will make her fascinated about you.

When you communicate confidently, boldly, with the assumption that everyone there is completely interested in what you have to say, you're going to notice something.

You're going to notice women looking at you. Not looking at you with glazed over boredom, but rather look at you with *those eyes*. Yes, the ones that say there is something very interesting in front of her. Something she wants to learn more about.

You might be thinking, *I talk to women 1-on-1. I give presentations. I speak in front of groups sometimes.* There are women in the audience. But I'm pretty sure I didn't get *those eyes* from any of them.

You probably didn't.

Are you nervous? Are you filtering? What is your body language like? You were probably not demonstrating great communication.

So start making a conscious effort to improve that. Everything in this course, from the Carefree Man belief system to the conversational techniques will help you accomplish this.

Still not sure where to start, then start by speaking without a filter.

Speaking with a filter (i.e. hiding what you really mean) is a great way to be a boring, shitty communicator. Filtering is boring. Boring is shitty communication.

There is only one "professional speaker" in your life, and that's you. You may not be presenting to auditoriums filled with spectators, but you should approach every conversation like you are.

You want to dazzle women with your stories.

Dazzling means working on the confidence behind your delivery. It means working on your pauses. It means working on your hand gestures and animation. It means chances in pitch and volume. It means talking faster and slower.

It means delivering punch lines with flamboyance and charisma.

To summarize: (1) be aware of it, (2) make an effort to actively improve it, and (3) practice.

Practicing is the most important part. And if you're following the Action Steps in this course, you will be talking to women.

That's a perfect time to practice.

Also, one of the exercises in 7 Mental Exercises to Get You Laid is making a list of 20 new descriptive words to incorporate into your vocabulary. This is a simple task that will help bring your communication to a whole new level.

Female Awareness

Demonstrating Female Awareness basically means demonstrating everything we talked about in the chapter: 'How Women Work.'

You are aware that most guys try to make logical conversation (basically logical arguments why they are a good candidate for a women's affections).

You're aware of it, and you don't do it.

You are aware that attraction is not linear. You don't talk in a linear fashion. You change it up. You move around from topic to topic. You keep her on her toes.

You know the signs to look for when women are attracted to men. You can demonstrate this by people watching *with* the woman you're attracting.

For example, let's say you two are at the bar.

You can notice another couple and say: "Look at those two over there. What do you think? Is she into him?"

Then you two can start picking the interaction apart together. Where are her shoulders pointing. Is he leaning in too much (needy). Is he leaning away (non-needy). What are their facial expressions like? Is she tapping her foot like she's ready to make a b-line to…..well anywhere away from this guy? Does this guy look as about exciting as a hamster?

As you two are picking this situation appart, you are demonstrating female awareness.

You're stories can include references that demonstrate this as well. Again, it's not the point of the story, it's just something casually mentioned that demonstrates female awareness.

For example, you're telling a story about being at the gym with your friend Hannah and a dude was hitting on her.
You could tell she was totally not into it, but the dude would just not go away.

So you walked over there and, ignoring the other guys presence, said to her: "sweetheart, I'm gonna stop by the store on the way home. I've got broccoli, steak, aspirin and tampons on my list. Anything else you want me to pick up baby?"

Then she (smiling) was like "no sweetheart, thank you. But hey can you spot me once before you go." Which you did. Meanwhile, Mr. Annoying sulked away in the background.

See, you just demonstrated female awareness. You also demonstrated preselection (by telling a story that included a female friend - bonus).

More on Body Language

In Phase 3 you want to employ the following body language techniques:

- When you're talking to her (telling her stories), you want to be making strong eye contact 80% to 100% of the time. Basically, when you're talking, you're looking at her (most of the time). That's reaching in with eye contact.

- When she's talking to you (telling you stories), you want to be making strong eye contact 60% to 80% of the time. Basically, when she's talking, you're looking at her, but you're also looking away, glancing around, etc. That's <u>withdrawing</u> with eye contact.

- When you're talking to her (telling her stories), you want to be leaning <u>toward</u> her slightly, 80% to 100% of the time. Basically, when you're talking, you're leaning in slightly (say a few degrees from standing straight up and down). That's <u>reaching in</u> with body posture.

- When she's talking to you (telling you stories), you want to be leaning <u>away from</u> her slightly, 80% to 100% of the time. Basically, when she's talking, you're leaning away (say a few degrees from standing straight up and down). That's <u>withdrawing</u> with body posture.

Everything is seduction is some for of reach and withdraw, push and pull, give and take away. Don't get hung up on the percentages above, just work on implementing the general concepts.
The reason I bring this up in Phase 3 rather than Phase 2 is because of the following.

In Phase 2, the conversation is a much quicker "back and forth." If you were leaning in and out with every change in who was talking, you'd look like one of those air-bag clowns that auto dealerships put out on the front curb.

So in Phase 2, don't worry about this, just focus on the fun, challenging and playful banter discussed in Chapter 5.

However in Phase 3, each person will be talking for longer periods of time while the other person is listening. This allows you to lean in slowly as you talk, and then lean out slowly as she starts talking.

Just be aware of it, and practice it. It won't be perfect at the beginning. If you find yourself in a situation where she's talking and you realize you're leaning in and looking at her too much, don't panic. Just slowly lean back, and start glancing away a little bit.

Do it all with slow alpha movements even if the timing is a little off.

Back to topics for story telling:

Fun, Positive and Challenging Emotions

We've gone over this one a lot. We know this is the fundamental secret to making women irresistibly attracted to you.

Let's just be clear that this is not limited to how you're acting in the moment. How you're acting "now" when talking to a woman.

It should be demonstrated within your stories as well.

First. All stories should have fun and positive vibes to them.

Second. They should (when possible) demonstrate that you were challenging to the people in the story.

For example, you're telling a story about bungee jumping in South Carolina.

Obviously that will be a fun story with a positive experience. If not then you shouldn't tell it. It should also be a story filled with emotions (all your stories should demonstrate emotions).

So how do you demonstrate that you are a challenging person.

Let's say the jump instructor asked everyone if they wanted the bungee to be attached to their backs or their feet. As the instructor is going from one person to the next, people are just deciding: *back, feet, back, etc.*

When the instructor gets to you, you started asking a bunch of questions. Which way is the most fun?

Which way gives the biggest rush? Maybe you insisted you couldn't decide here on the ground, so you want to take up both types of harnesses, and decide after you see other people jump various ways.

Again, the point of the story is not that you're challenging the instructor. The point is that you wanted to have a specific, wild experience that was full of emotion. And you were going to do what it took to make the best decision for yourself. You wanted the best experience possible. And while getting that for yourself, you just happened to be challenging to someone else.

Another example might be: someone doesn't want to do something for you. Instead of taking no for an answer, you are challenging and convince them to do it anyway.

Any story that involves you teasing women and making them laugh, demonstrates that you are fun, positive and challenging.

You Demonstrating That You're Are Improving Yourself Daily

This is any story that involves you learning something new or improving yourself physically. We've used the yoga class reference a lot in this training. Yoga, gym, cycling, hiking, any kind of physical activity that you're newly undertaking (or maybe not newly, but undertaking more seriously) demonstrates this.

As part of this course you should be taking 15 minutes per day to learn about some new topic. Any story that involves any of these new topics demonstrates this.

You Demonstrating Preselection

We've gone over this a lot. Any story that involves you interacting with, being with, or helping (or them helping you) women demonstrates this.

One last clarifying point about preselection. Some guys mistakenly think that if a girl sees them or hears about them with other women that she will lose interest. Or think he's taken, or something like that.

That is 100% backwards. Women want guys that other women want. Write that down if you need to. Do everything you can to tell stories, display on social media, and just generally be seen with women.

Also remember that the point is not that you know women. The point of the story is something else, and women just happen to be there.

You Demonstrating High Social Status

In some ways this is similar to demonstrating Leadership.

In Leadership you're demonstrating how people respond to you as a leader. Here you are demonstrating how people respond to you in general, even if you're not the leader.

Your stories should demonstrate that other people value your opinion. Other people care about what you say. Other people take your advice and achieve success following that advice.

How to Bring Your Stories To Life

Nicknames and Backstories.

Everyone in your stories should have nicknames and backstories. Both of these things will instantly make the listener feel like she can relate to the characters in the story. It gives something she can make a connection with.

Let's say you're telling the story about when your friend Clara introduced you to this new diet book that you're reading.

So you're like:

"...so Clairol calls me up freaking out. By the way her name is Clara, but I call her Clairol because seriously her hair is a different color like...pretty much weekly. So anyway, she calls me and starts going off about the dangers of beef and chicken and....."

Here you used a nickname and a tiny backstory (that she's a hair color nut) which gives the character a relatable, emotional connection. The woman you're talking to probably has a friend who colors her hair all the time too.

This helps the whole story come to life.

Now Clara is not some generic female avatar who is worried about carcinogens in beef and ranting about a new diet.

She's now a woman with crimson, aqua and pumpernickel hair, nicknamed Clairol, who's worried about carcinogens in beef.

Conflict

All great stories have conflict. This doesn't mean war. This doesn't mean violence. It just means some conflict between characters.

So let's say you're continuing with the Clairol story and you're like:

"...yeah and then Clairol told her roommate Stephanie about the book. By the way Stephie comes from this honky-type family that always wears shirts saying stuff like: Eat. Sleep. Hunt. Repeat.

Anyway, after she tells Stefs about the book, Stefs goes out and buys a dozen porterhouse steaks that filled the freezer.

Clairol was so pissed that apparently she cooked all the steaks and fed them to the neighbor's dogs. I'm not sure what happened after that but it's gonna be interesting...."

Pause for Dramatic Effect

This is a great skill for storytelling. This is a great skill for anytime you're speaking.
Pausing helps you slow down and creates suspense.

Recall that the first step to developing alpha male body language is to slow down.

The most confident speakers always pause. Great places to pause are at high points and cliffhangers. Pause right before something dramatic is going to happen.

Now that you're aware of this, you will start to notice that most people rush when they talk. They talk like there's some verbal race going on and whoever finishes first gets the prize.

But it's actually the exact opposite.

Rushing makes you seem less confident in what you're saying and it makes the story less interesting.

Pausing may feel a little awkward when you first start practicing, but it's critical to great speech and great storytelling.

When you really get good at it, you can pause for a really long time. A playfully long time. To the point where the listener is chomping at the bit, waiting to hear what happens next. .

Be Animated with Your Stories

This means change your vocal tone. Change your volume. Move your arms for dramatic effect (not with twitchy, flighty beta movements; but with intentional, calculated alpha movements).

Make facial expressions that emphasize the emotions of your story.

Do all of this with slow, deliberate movements. Stick to the body language principles we discussed earlier in Make Women Chase You. But become animated. Show her your emotional side.

High Investment Questions

In addition to stories, asking questions that get her to reveal deeper, personal information is a great way to create an emotional connection.

Low Investment vs High Investment - This is a simple concept you should understand from what we've gone through already, but just in case:

The more she reveals about herself. The more vulnerable she makes herself (by revealing personal information), the higher investment she is making in you.

Revealing her name, that she's from Akron and the she likes ballet is low investment. It's not too personal. She's not too vulnerable.

Revealing her deeply held beliefs about animal cruelty, family ties, and relationships is high investment. It's more personal and it makes her more vulnerable.

Examples of High Investment Questions:

- So were you scared [when you did whatever] as a kid?   Like what were the feelings you can remember about going there?"
- If you could change one thing (about yourself, about the world, about college education, about any 'large' topic), what would it be?
- What's something outside of your comfort zone you've always wanted to do?
- What's one important thing I should know about you?

The theme in all of these is feelings, emotions, opinions about large topics, comfort zones, personal information.

When to drop these?

Drop them randomly just like anything else. Drop them anytime you're in Phase 3 - Attraction.

What if I'm not sure that I'm in Phase 3?

Do it like this. Always start with stories. You're building curiosity in Phase 2, everything is lite and playful. Then something is said which causes a story to be shared. Maybe she shares a story. Then you share some personal relatable story.

Once you're seeing stories being shared, you're in Phase 3. Feel free to drop one of these High Investment Questions anytime.

Moving Around The Venue

When a woman spends time with you in different locations, it creates the illusion of knowing you longer.

The illusion occurs even if you're moving to different locations within the same venue. The view is different in a new location. The people standing around are different. Maybe it's a switch from bar stools to a table, or to a lounge area.

You don't need to go overboard, but switching locations with a girl during Phase 3 is a good thing to do. Just make sure it's your idea. When she agrees, it further demonstrates that you're in charge of the conversation.

Just say "hey, let's move over here second." Then just take her by the hand and go. It wasn't a question. Assume everything.

So you get compliance on her part, and you get the added benefit of spending time with her in two (or more) locations. If she feels like she has known you longer, it makes escalation that much easier.

*****

It's time to take action.

Over the next week or so, complete all the exercises in Daytime Unleashed. Power through them. Review the conversation techniques in Chapters 5 and 6. Pick one to three techniques that you really like and just practice them everyday with each Action Step.

Focus on completing the Action Steps, no matter what. The outcome of any step is irrelevant. Every time you do one, you are learning so much through taking action, which is the most important thing.

Keep it up. You're doing amazing!!

Chapter 7: Attraction Phase 4 – Captivation

Before reading this chapter, go to your bonus supplement How To Touch Women and read that first.

It's All About The Close

What's the difference between guys who are *pretty good* with women, and guys who get laid all the time?

It's the close.

You have to close. Everything up to this point is meaningless if you never close.

We've all heard the phrase, "always be closing." Well get used to it. If you want to have a flood of women in your life, you will need to close.

Remember what I said at the beginning of this course. Women *will* chase men. Women *will* chase **you**. But there are two things women won't do: (1) Women won't chase strangers. So you have to initiate. Women won't make the initial close (usually). So you have to close.

Here's the part about "the close" that most guys don't realize:

The close is ongoing. The close *is not* a one time event.

Think about closing from an auto dealership perspective. Is it a one time event? No. First they close you on a vehicle, then they close on options, then they close on financing, then later they start closing you on service, then a while later they start closing you on selling your car back to them and buying a new one.   It goes on and on. It doesn't stop.

Think about closing from a cruise line perspective. They close you on a specific cruise. Then on stateroom choices. Then drink packages. Then shore excursions. Then before you even finish the first cruise, they're trying to close you on booking another cruise.

You should see from these examples that "always be closing" does not mean: close person 1 with a one-time event, then close person 2 with a one-time event, then close person 3 with a one-time event.

Instead it means close the same person over and over and over. Incremental closes. Progressive closes. Close for one thing. Then close for the next thing.

Also note that the best progressive closing happens with the two steps forward, one step back approach. It happens with reach and withdraw. Otherwise it's smothering.

The best auto dealerships and cruise lines do this. They try to close you on something, but if you don't bite, they change the subject and tell you about something else that perhaps isn't a close -- just something interesting for you to know about. They back up a little, give you some room, make you their friend by giving you more information about something else, and then try to close again later.

It's exactly the same with women. You close on a small thing. You change the subject. You keep up the fun, playful and challenging vibe. You close on the next small thing. You pull. You push. You go forward and then you back up.

So as you implement the guidance in this course into your life, you are progressively closing already. Each step forward that you take (like going from upper back touching to lower back touching) is a small close.

Knowing this should make your realize that closing for the number, closing for the kiss, closing for second base, closing for the lay; these are all just small incremental closes.

They are not humongous closing hurdles which must be feared and struggled to overcome. They are just part of moving two steps forward, and then backing up.

Certain incremental closes can also be direct (like asking for her number) or they can be indirect (like making getting her number - not the goal - but simply a logistical necessity). We'll do an example of this shortly.

With these ideas in mind, let's look at incremental closing in different situations.

Daytime

Attracting women during the day is generally a much shorter process than at night. You will generally get to only Curiosity (Phase 2). You have to get here obviously. After all, if she's not at least curious, there's no reason to give you her number, FB or Snap.

Her investment in you is low. The conversation is enough to spark curiosity, but not enough to build an emotional connection. There most likely hasn't been any touching, other than a handshake.

In this case the best option (only option really) is to do a direct close. Just ask for her number, FB or Snap.

If this is a college or work situation, go for the FB or Snap under the premise that you're just building your social network. Remember that we never direct close in environments where we're going to see that person again.

Assuming it's an "out in the world" situation and you will never see this woman again, ask for the number.

"Hey let me get your number, I'd like to take you out some time." Hand her your phone.

"Hey I'd like to take you out for a coffee sometime. What do you say?" Hand her your phone.

Simple.

You'll kick yourself in the ass for the rest of the day if you talk to a woman for 5 minutes and forget to close for the number. So don't make that mistake. Go for it, just to see what happens.

If you've built enough curiosity in the 5 minutes you've spoken to her, she'll most likely give you the number.

Getting a number during the day generally leads to dates at night, and this is where more subtle, progressive closing occurs.

Nighttime

When you're following approaches laid out in this course, you should be able to build the attraction up to Captivation.

This means she is beyond fascinated with you. She is giving you her full attention with her eyes and with her body language. She's laughing at all your jokes. She's moved locations with you in the venue. She's twirling her hair. She's biting her lip. You've escalated touching to the point where you're hands are at least, on her hips, the side of her ass.

If you've arrived at this point, then this girl is captivated by you. But remember what I mentioned earlier about women responding differently to you now that you're implementing the strategies in this course.

I said it was easy to fall back into old routines. It was easy to let her take charge of the situation or start putting her back up on a pedestal. Well, it's also easy to get too eager. Especially when this is all happening for the first time.

If you're hands are all over her and her eyes are all over you, and the vibe "is there," you might be eager to close for going home together.

My recommendation is that you don't close for going home together the night you meet.

Yes you can certainly try it. Yes it can work. Yes there are women out there who will sleep with you on the first night. But I recommend this alternative instead:

As you transform into the highest version of yourself, the version this course is guiding you to become, you will have lots of women chasing after you.

And what do women chase? They chase things they can't have. They chase men who are "above them," who have a "higher status" than they do. Just like everyone chases things that they can't have and are above them.

A women might go home with you on the first night, she might sleep with you, but she often will lose all fascination with you in the morning. She often will regret sleeping with you and you won't hear from her again. That's why they're called one night stands. Because if you LET a women sleep with you the night you meet her, it shows you're not really that "high status." That you really don't have that many choices when it comes to women. That you're too easy to get. And the bubble of captivation bursts.

And let's be honest, sex in the first few months of dating a woman (after you get to know what each other likes in bed) is way better than sex on the first night

So when her eyes are all over you, and your hands are all over her, and the vibe "is there," here's what I recommend instead:

Take it away.

She will be shocked. She will be dumbfounded. She will have that feeling of longing for something that was there and is now gone. Her attraction to you will spike into the red zone and she will be prepared to do anything to get your attention back. Believe me, the next time you see her, she will be coming onto you super strong.

Here's how you do it:

First, while you're both in this bubble of captivation. When she's googly-eyeing you and you're hands are all over her. When all the noise and commotion around you in the venue seems blurry, distant and faded. When you two are in your own little world.

At that point, tell her a story of a date that the two of you are going to go on in the future.

You don't have to put any specifics around it as far as dates and times. Just describe a fascinating date that will happen at some undetermined future time. See your bonus 7 Mental Exercises to Get You Laid, for instructions on how to describe your Go To Date.

Tell her that story. Make it sound uber-exciting, like it would be the funnest experience she's ever had. Really build up the anticipation. Describe it in vivid detail. Make her think "wow I would love to do all of this with this guy."

Your voice should be slow and deep. Remember, talking slower naturally makes your voice deeper. So just slow down. Take your time. She's captivated by you. Own it. Let her relish in being entranced by a dominant alpha male.

You should have a slight playful smirk. She might blush a little and her eyes might flinch away if you're looking at her intensely. Make sure your eyes don't flinch away.

When you're done describing the date, just stare off into space for a few beats, like you're really thinking about it. Like you're really thinking about all the detail.

This gives her the chance to really think about it too. To let it sink in. She won't say anything. She will just be entranced.

Then abruptly look back at her and change the subject.

You can change the subject to anything but ideally you want to make it something that creates a physical connection. See your bonus How To Touch Women.

Here's some examples:

If you did the palm reading earlier, you can go back to that. If you didn't do it, now is a great time. Either way, take her hands and go into a silly "reading."

If you did it earlier: "Hey let me see your palms one more time."

If you didn't then : "You know, I never told you, I'm actually a world famous palm reader. Here, let me see your hands."

Take her hands. Assume everything.

For example:

"Oh yes……..um…….yes it says here that you are going to go on a marvelous date with a strapping young stud.

Yes, you will wear a beautiful summer dress that will flow delicately in the even breeze as you stroll along the boardwalk.

The gulls will be calling in the distance. The waves will be lapping at the shore.

The…..oh wait…..hmmmm...yes it says you will purchase a small plate of french fries, extra ketchup, from a vending cart.

But then the wind will pick up and you will spill the fries all over yourself. The extra ketchup will make the fries stick all over your summer dress.

The exposed fries will cause us to be attacked by a swarm of wild pigeons which will chase us furiously until we dive for cover behind a lemonade stand…….”

Etc.

The point of doing this is to get her laughing hard.

And while this story might seem absurd (which it is), remember that you have her mesmerized inside of your private bubble.

At that moment, you can say anything ridiculous in the world and she will love it. And she will laugh her ass off.

As soon as you have her laughing hysterically (even if the story isn't finished), you abruptly stop, and take all the fun emotions away.

Pull out your phone quickly, like you suddenly realized something, and say "Oh crap, I've got to go."

Maybe you're late for meeting up with some friends. You promised your sister you would come over late that night and help her with something. You have a big presentation at work tomorrow that you forgot to prepare for. It doesn't really matter.

"Oh crap, I've got to go....I totally forgot I told my buddy Jessie I would meet him at (wherever) at (whenever)."

Her face will drop. You will see it. From completely hysterical to. *What? You're leaving?* She will be stunned. Complete disbelief.

.

As this is registering in her mind, you say: "But we're totally going to [whatever the date was that you described before].

Hand her your phone. "Here, put your number in there so we can set it up."

Total assumption. No hesitation.

If you've done everything we've discussed above. She'll put her number right in there, no questions asked.

When she hands the phone back, you pull her in for a hug. Hold for a second or two too long, and then back away. Maintain strong eye contact. Have a smirk that says you're just a little too confident.

When you're a foot or two away: "I'll see you later."

Turn and go.

That's it.

You have successfully built up huge anticipation and made getting the number merely a secondary, logistical thing.

She will be thinking about you constantly and craving the text you will send her to arrange the date.

*****

Text her the next day and tell her it was great to meet her and you're looking forward to the upcoming date.

Don't spend much time texting. If she asks anything back, keep your responses short and to the point. Then give her two options of nights your free. Arrange the date and end the conversation.

Don't text her again. Wait for the date.

Take her on the Go To date you described. Have a blast. Start over in Phase 2 building curiosity. Then build fascination. There should be lots of playful (Phase 2 banter during the date) and mixed in should more emotional connection building.

Start at the beginning with touching as well, and progressively move forward.

You're essentially doing the same progressive closing over again, except this time on a date. And this time it will be much smoother and move much quicker.

Toward the end of the date you want to lean in for the kiss. Another progressive close.

There are two basic things to look for right before leaning in for the kiss. Either she's laughing a lot. Or she's talking a lot.

With either of these you can do the "pause/seductive approach" or the "interrupter approach." For example:

Pause/seductive approach: Wait for a high note when she's laughing. Then pause. Look at her seductively with strong eye contact. Watch her as she recovers from laughing. There will be a silent pause here where she sees you looking at her but not saying anything. Don't let the pause linger for more than one or two beats.

Then just reach up, put your hand on the back of her neck and pull her (lightly) halfway to you. You lean in the other half way. Put your mouth on hers and kiss. Do it without hesitation.

Interrupter approach: Let's she's talking a lot late in the date. She's kind of rambling on and on. Often this means she wants to kiss you, but is nervous.

Don't wait for her to finish. Don't wait for her to come to a pause. Just lean in all the way in and kiss her. Just put you mouth onto her mouth right in the middle of her talking. No hesitation. Assume everything.

*****

Next steps.

If you haven't yet completed the Action Steps in Daytime Unleashed, continue moving forward. Then move to Nighttime Unleashed and complete that part of the course.

Continue moving forward with the exercises in 7 Mental Exercises to Get You Laid. Take these seriously. Write down the stories you need to fascinate and captivate women and make those stories your own. Practice telling them with all the techniques we discussed in the course.

Reread Chapters 5 and 6 of this course as necessary until your conversation becomes free flowing, confident and endless.

Practice touching women. Review the guide How To Touch Women. Take it slow. You don't have to implement every touching strategy on the first attempt.

Start with only the "public area" touching for a while until it becomes natural. Until it becomes part of the way you communicate. Then add in one more touch. Then one more.

If you've reached this point, you've built up a lot of momentum. Keep it up. Keep approaching and building attraction with women. Make a goal to approach women randomly several times a week.

Do it just for the sake of doing it. Do it just to keep up the momentum. Remember that you don't have to build a lifelong relationship with every women you talk to. You don't have to even call them again. So just approach and build attraction to stay sharp. To stay prepared.

That way, when that rare opportunity comes along. When the unicorn comes prancing by someday. You'll be ready. Because you won't find the unicorn on Tinder, Bumble or online.

One day, the unicorn will just walk by.

And if you're not ready……..

Supplement Course 1: Daytime Unleashed

(25 Day Action Plan to Change Your Life – Part 1)

In the next 25 days you're literally going to see yourself transform into the chick attraction magnet you've always wanted to be.

Here's how to use this action plan. Read Make Women Chase You first. The guidebook will instruct you when to stop reading and come here to the supplement to complete an Action Step.

So if you opened this first, and haven't looked at Make Women Chase You yet. Close this supplement now, and go to the main guidebook.

Do these steps need to be completed in exactly 25 days? No.

The steps will require you to be in certain situations. Obviously, this may not work out perfectly with your schedule, etc. At the same time, we don't want to drag things out too long.

One of the biggest ways to achieve success is through momentum. You start building momentum and it carries you through to the finish. If you wait too long in between Action Steps, you lose momentum.

So shoot to complete one Action Step everyday. But let's put in some buffer days to be realistic. Try to complete all the Action Steps within 25 to 50 days.

Just make sure to do the Action Steps in order. They build on each other, so don't skip around.

Why Most Guys Fail

Before we start, let's discuss the #1 reason why people try and fail (at anything, not just attracting women). It's because of this:

Too Much Information.

Really.

There's just too much information out there. It's information overload really. And that causes paralysis of analysis.

You can spend the rest of your life reading about seduction. But reading will get you nowhere.

This course is designed to weed through all the noise and give you concrete, actionable steps. <u>The most important thing is that you do them</u>.

Most of these (particularly in Daytime Unleashed) should take an hour or less. You can do them on your lunch break, so no excuses, get them done.

Here's <u>what not to worry about</u> as you go through these Action Steps:

1. Don't worry if this is "the best" line or "the best" approach.

There is *no* best line or best approach. A guy who knows how to seduce women can take the most dog shit line in the world and pull it off everytime. A guy who has no clue can take a great line and screw it up every time.

It is not the line. It is the man. Remember that. Over the next 25 days you will determine which lines you like and which you don't.

The ones you like you'll keep, perfect and make your own. The others you'll toss.

2. Don't worry about the outcome. We care about seeing what happens. Not about outcomes.

Let's begin.

Action Step 1: Hit on a Waitress to See What Happens

A waitress is the easiest place to start. Why? Because waitresses are in customer service. They will be nice to you even if they turn you down. This should immediately eliminate any concerns you have about a harsh rejection.

So now, there's really nothing to worry about.

Very important: You're not hitting on a waitress because you want to sleep with her. You're not hitting on her because you want any specific outcome. **You're only hitting on her TO SEE WHAT HAPPENS.**

Right? Fuck it.

Here are the exact steps to take. Go somewhere and get a female waitress. Talk to her as much as you can when ordering and throughout the meal. In other words, don't just order and then be quiet.

One thing you must do to satisfy this exercise is: You must make at least 1 Assumption about her. Something like this:

"You seem like a Cali girl to me."
"You seem like you're from New York."

"You look like you're into yoga."
"You look like you're really into fitness."

You can use one of those, or ideally, say whatever actually comes to mind the moment you see her (no filter -- whatever you think the moment you see her -- just say it -- you seem like a [whatever] girl to me).

Say it right away. Like:

Her: "Hi I'm Brenda, I'll be your server."
You: "Hi Brenda. How's it going today?"
Her: [she says whatever]
You: "You know...you seem like a [whatever] girl to me."
Her: [she will most certainly ask why, or why do you think that]
You: "I'm not sure. I'm just getting that [whatever] vibe from you. I'll think about it while I look over the menu. Got any specials today?

That's it.

She may ask you about the assumption again (girls generally do). **Just keep deflecting:** You're still not sure. It's just something about her. You're still trying to figure out what it is. But you're definitely going to put your finger on it by the end of the meal.

After deflecting, just change the subject (and really try to keep her engaged in conversation as much as possible -- obviously she's busy so it won't be forever -- but just keep it up as much as you can).

Things to change the subject to (if they haven't been covered in the conversation with her already):

- Ask her what her name is (if she doesn't have a name tag on or introduce herself).
- If she does have a name tag on, look at it for a beat. Then say her name. Then say nice to meet you.
- Ask her how her day is going.
- Ask her how long she's worked there.
- Ask her about something in the restaurant. Like some unusual decoration or picture or whatever hanging on the wall.
- Tell her you've never seen her in here before. (If she says she's never see *you* in here before: Tell her that's because *you've* never been here before. Then give her a wink and a smirk and look back at your menu.)
- Ask her what the most popular dish is.
- Ask her what her favorite dish is.
- Ask her if she can describe the difference between Dish 1 and Dish 2.

You don't have to use every one of these. Pick one or two and change the subject so the cliffhanger of your assumption is just sitting out there.

Talk to her calmly with genuine interest. If she responds with anything that keeps the conversation going, just go with it. It doesn't matter what you say.

If you're ever stuck, you can always turn the conversation back to food.

Be playful and happy and a little teasing. Say everything in this interaction with confidence. Assume confidence. Assume this girl wants you. Remember, you're just doing all this to see what happens.

When the meal is over and she brings the check, she will probably be demanding to know why you assumed that thing about her.

If she is, say: I'll tell you what. You go for coffee with me this weekend, and I'll tell you.

If she isn't pressing for it. Just say: "Your service has been awesome. So awesome actually that I want to take you out for a coffee this weekend."

That's it.

It doesn't matter what happens after that.

If she reacts favorably, just go with it. Say whatever comes naturally. Then hand her your phone.

If she says no or that she has a boyfriend or whatever, just say: "Totally cool. I understand. Thanks again for the awesome service and conversation."

Done.

Things to Keep in Mind

In general, these will be applicable to all the Action Steps.

1. Don't spend forever finding "the right" waitress. Your goal is to get in, complete the Action Step, get out, and move on with the training. So, if the server (a) is female, (b) isn't wearing a wedding band, and (3) isn't someone clearly out of your age range (like a grandma), then she's "the right" waitress for this exercise.

2. To be totally clear on the previous point. You don't have to marry this women. You don't even have to call her if you get the number. You're not committing to anything. So even if she's not "the ideal candidate" for you, just complete the Action Step. Don't overthink things. You're going to hit on girls in this course, just for the sake of hitting on girls (just to see what happens). You don't ever have to follow up if you don't want to.

3. Don't worry if other people are within earshot. Who cares. You will never see those people again. If you're still concerned about it, go to a restaurant that's noisy. Nobody will hear you anyway.

4. When you're done. When you're in your car (or wherever) outside the restaurant. Take a moment to notice and acknowledge how exhilarated you feel. It will feel good (no matter what happened). And this is only the beginning.

Lastly, I recommend doing this Action Step solo. However, if you're with a buddy, just do everything the same way. But here's the one key. Don't tell your buddy what you're doing. Just let him witness it live. If you tell him in advance, his face will give away that hitting on her wasn't spontaneous.

OK. Stop reading here. Go complete this Action Step. Then go back to Make Women Chase You, and pick up with Chapter 3.

Action Step 2: Hit on a Waitress with the "I didn't see your number" line and See What Happens

This time you will do everything you did in Action Step 1, except the ending. So go back and review all the suggestions of what to talk about in Action Step 1.

Make sure you make an assumption about her, and then defer telling her why for the entire meal.

Remember it's very important to talk to her as much as possible. You don't want to go from "hey can I have the spinach salad" to "hey can I have your number." You want to talk with her as much as possible in between those things.

The difference this time will be the close. This time you will drop a funny pick up line. Trust me this one works wonders because it's totally unexpected and funny.

Here's how it works.

Let her drop off the check. Take your normal few minutes to look it over. When she comes back say: "hey, there's uh...something wrong with my check."

You should have a mildly skeptical/concerned look on your face (the look that would be on your face if there *really was* something wrong with the check).

You should actually hand the check to her as you're saying the line above.

She will certainly take the check from you. And she will probably say something like "oh no" or "omg what's wrong" or something like that.

As soon as she has the check in her hand, you continue with: "I didn't see your number written at the top."

Then just stop. Look at her. Sly smile/half smirk on your face. Total confidence. Total assumption.

There will be one or two beats while her mind processes that you just hit on her. Then she will either bust out laughing or (at a minimum) she will get a big smile.

This is always the reaction because the line was so unexpected after you framed it as something was wrong with the check.

After that, just go with whatever happens. Give her a few seconds to respond. If she's completely lost (which is unlikely), you can ask her: "has anyone ever asked you out like that before?" (The answer will most certainly be no).

If you get the number, great!

If she give you boyfriends and excuses, use this exit:

"Totally cool. I understand. You can't blame me for trying though right? (she will surely say no). Nice. Thanks for being a good sport about it. And thanks again for the great service. You have an awesome day."

That's it.

Make sure to take note of how exhilarated you feel afterwards, regardless of the outcome.

Again, you just did it to see what happens.

OK. Stop reading here. Go complete this Action Step. Then go back and pick up Make Women Chase You, and pick up with Chapter 4.

Action Step 3: Compliment a Girl on the Street with "I Think You're Absolutely Gorgeous" and See What Happens

For this one, go somewhere that's kind of a "big" public place. This would be like a busy boardwalk, a mall, a crowded part of town. The opposite of this would be like a small coffee shop or a quiet bookstore. There should be lots of people wandering around doing whatever.

What you're going to do here is give a stranger a compliment. That's it. You're not hitting on anyone. You're not looking for any particular outcome.

What happens after the compliment doesn't matter. Your only job is to deliver a compliment and meet these requirements:

The compliment you're going to give is this: "Excuse me. I just wanted to tell you that I think you are absolutely gorgeous."

The requirements you have to meet are: You have to say the compliment with a strong, calm, confident voice. Confident body language. Strong eye contact. And a smile.

Let's break these down.

A strong, calm, confident, voice is one that isn't hiding, timid or scared. It's a voice that isn't rushing through the words. This is a gorgeous women. You need to tell her that and make her genuinely believe it.

You should practice that line beforehand until it flows out of your mouth calmly and confidently, without any hesitation or thought.

Confident body language is when you walk toward her, you walk with purpose. Purpose doesn't mean a fast or running. It means no hesitation. No second guessing. You're going to deliver this compliment come hell or high water.

Strong eye contact means you look at her in the eye when you deliver the line. And you DON'T break eye contact after you deliver the line. Look at her in the eyes like you can see into her soul.

A smile -- give her your best.

Here is exactly how you're going to accomplish this to minimize any anxiety.

You're going to have an *ON* and *OFF* mode. *Off* mode is safe and comfortable, because you're not hitting on anybody, even if you see a hot chick. The reason to be in *off* mode is so you don't start creating anxiety on the drive over there, and when you first get there, etc.

In *off* mode you're just an everyday dude going about his business. Nothing can happen until you turn to *on* mode.

Once you get to this place, wander around for a few minutes in *off* mode. Check out the shops. Check out the beach. Check out whatever. Take notice of hot chicks just like any guy normally would. You're just noticing, you're not doing anything yet.

Now, very similar to the restaurant example, you're not looking for "the perfect hot girl."

If you keep looking for the perfect one, you'll be there all day and never accomplish anything.

You just need to spot a "good enough hot girl", who is walking/shopping alone. Remember you're just completing an exercise here. Nothing more. The rest of your life is not hanging in the balance.

The moment you see a "good enough hot girl." The moment you're sure she's alone (like she's not busy talking to some store clerk). You whisper to yourself: "on mode. fuck it." Then you start walking toward her, no thinking, no hesitation.

As soon as you get to her you deliver the line.

When you say "Excuse me." Say it like a statement. Not a question. You're not asking her if you can have her attention. You're telling her that she's going to give you her attention for the next few moments.

Then deliver the line. Then pause. Smile. Hold that eye contact (do not for the love of God break eye contact - I don't care how hard your heart is pounding).

Most likely, she will get a big smile. She will probably say thank you. Any person who can't take a genuine compliment is just an asshole.

If she says thank you, you say: "You're welcome. I just couldn't resist coming over and talking to you. I'm Paul. Who are you?"

Hold out your hand.

"Nice to meet you Sasha. So, what are you up to today?"

She says something.

You make an assumption about her. Whatever comes to mind, or use one of the assumptions you've seen repeatedly throughout the course.

Defer answering. Change the subject. Check out the conversations in Chapter 5 of Make Women Chase You. Pick out a few go-to lines and practice them in advance.

If she asks what you're up to (since you're up to nothing but hitting on chicks). Just say: "I'm meeting a buddy at 3:00 over at [some place nearby] so I was just doing some window shopping. Killing some time."

If things start getting awkward or she doesn't seem interested. Your out is: "hey, it looks like you have a lot to do. It was nice to meet you. You have a great day!" Said with total confidence.

Then turn slowly and confidently and walk away. Don't look back.

If she does seem interested in you, ask for her number. Don't drag it out too long. Always be closing. After even just a minute or two say:

"Hey look I really want to take you out. Let me get your number so we can go out and have some fun." Hold out your phone for her to take.

Reflect on how exhilarated you feel as you walk away. Doesn't matter the outcome. You were just there to see what happened. And if you happened to get a hottie's number...well holy fuck stud. Nice work.

Action Step 4: Hit on a Girl with the "Hey You Dropped That" line and See What Happens

Go to a daytime venue where people are walking around. It can be the same place as in Action Step 3, or somewhere else. Just make sure lots of people are walking around.

Follow the same steps in Action Step 3. Be in *off* mode for a few minutes until you're ready to go.

You want this line in your arsenal because it's a great go-to when you and a woman are walking toward each other, and there's no time to think.

For example, let's say you round a corner, and there is a woman right there coming toward you, and you have only seconds to (1) decide to say something and (2) figure out what to say.

This line is perfect for those situations because you can drop it immediately no matter what is really going on.

For practice, you can do it when you and a woman are walking toward each other. Or you can just use it on a woman who is standing, let's say browsing a rack of clothing or something like that.

Here's how it works.

The moment you're within speaking distance from her, let's say less than 10 feet away, you just immediately look surprised and you point to the ground right behind her and say:

"Hey, you dropped that."

Pretend that she really did drop something, and your body and vocal tone will give off exactly the right signals.

Most of the time she will stop, turn around, and look at where you're pointing. That's just human nature. Nobody wants to drop their keys, or an important paper, or whatever. So if a stranger alerts you that you dropped something, you will look.

So she will look for a second or two, then she will look back at you confused. Because obviously there is nothing there.

At that moment, you say (with a big, confident smile): "I'm just kidding. I just needed a reason to stop you, so I can hit on you real quick."

At this point, one of two things will happen. She will either roll her eyes and walk away. Or, she'll smile/laugh and still be standing there.

If she's still standing there. You stick out your hand: "Hi. I'm Alfonzo. Who are you?"

Then go into the normal routine. Make an assumption. Defer the answer. Change the subject. Don't be afraid to mix in some questions depending on the situation:

"What are you up to today?"

"You go to school around here?"

"You work around here?"

"You on your lunch break?"

"Shoe shopping huh? How come you don't have any bags? No luck yet?"

"I'll tell you what. Let's go into that store right there (point at store) and you try on 3 pairs of shoes. And I'll give you my opinion."

Whatever. Just go with whatever she says. And make sure to ask for her number, snap, FB or whatever within a few minutes. At some random point just say:

"You seem really cool. Let me get your number so I can take you out later this week."

Close. Close. Close. If she's talking to you, you have to close.

If she gives you boyfriends and excuses, that's fine. If you close for the number and don't get it, that's fine.

But not attempting to close at all….that's not fine.

Review the conversation techniques in Chapter 5 of Make Women Chase You. Have 2 or 3 that you want to practice and try to implement them.

Very important: Don't overthink things. Don't worry about the outcome. You're just completing an exercise designed to get you to approach a random woman and say random stuff. You just need to get used to doing that. Once you can do that, everything else will fall into place. The outcome of this interaction is irrelevant. All that matters is that you make the approach.

Action Step 5: Marathon Day 1 - Hit on 2 Women In a Row To See What Happens

First, let me congratulate you for making it this far.

Most guys will do anything to improve their game, except actually approach women.

By doing what you did over the last 4 days, you have put yourself so far ahead of most guys. Be proud of what you've done. If you got rejected 4 times, who cares. You were just there to see what happens. Most guys will never do what you did.

Really.

Most guys will just live out their lives in quiet desperation, always wanting, always studying, and never obtaining, because the subconscious fight to "stay comfortable" is just too strong. They won't get uncomfortable and override it.

I'm glad to see you've made the conscious decision not to do that.

So….you have done awesome so far. But this Action Step can be a make or break moment. Don't let it stop you. Fight through this one. If you can get past this one, you really have a great chance of making it all the way to the end of this training and changing your life!

Here's the key. This one isn't any harder than yesterday. It just has the appearance of being harder because in involves 2 approaches in a row. And you have to be in *on* mode for a couple of minutes. Fight through this one and get it done. You'll be really happy that you did.

Here's how it works. Review the techniques in Action Step 3 & 4. You can use either technique or mix it up. If you have some other opening you want to try, use that.

Go to the public venue. Stay in off mode at the beginning.

When you see the first girl: *on* mode, "fuck it."

Approach the first girl. Open, introduce yourself, make an assumption, use the techniques from Chapter 5. Whatever happens doesn't matter.

As soon as you're done with the first approach, just keep walking around in *on* mode, until you see another hottie. Again, it doesn't have to be "the perfect hottie," just a "good enough hottie is fine."

Find a "good enough hottie" quickly. A couple of minutes max. As soon as you do, "fuck it" and approach. No thinking. No hesitation. Drop one of the openings. Follow the general pattern of assumption, defer the answer, change the subject.

The time might feel like forever when you're in *on* mode. But when it's done, it will feel like it went by really quickly. And you will feel glorious.

Last thing, do not spend one second worrying if the first girl might see you hitting on the second girl, or vice versa. Who cares. Now too long from now you're going to want girls to see you talking to other girls for preselection purposes.

So if the second "good enough hottie" is spotted 1 second after you depart the first "good enough hottie," go with it.

Remember: Two numbers, two rejections, or a mix of both. Doesn't matter!!! The fact that you did it is all that matters. All the women you want are coming. No one learned to ride a bike without bruising a few knees.

Action Step 6: Yoga Class

Find a yoga place that offers a free first lesson. If you're dude who's above yoga, get over yourself. Lots of buff dudes who get laid all the time by hotties in yoga pants, take yoga. So just do it.

I'm not telling you to become a yoga guru and spend the rest of your life doing yoga. I'm telling you to take one free yoga class.

Schedule the class. When you get there, you'll probably meet the instructor or someone that works there. You might be shown around. Whatever. There will probably be a few minutes of downtime before the class begins. Make sure to get there 20 minutes early so there is definitely a little down time.

During this time, there will be women around, stretching, prepping, whatever.

Your goal is to introduce yourself to 3 to 5 women during this time. This is one of the two primary reasons you're here (we'll get to reason 2 in a minute).

Just go up to them and introduce yourself. They will be friendly. Ideally it would be great if there were 5 women near each other. Just walk over, shake hands and exchange names with all of them. All in a row. They'll welcome you to the class. They might ask you if this is your first class. All good stuff.

Have a reason why you're interested in yoga. If you can't think of anything, just go with: "I'm always interested in trying new things."

Try to remember all 5 names. Repeat each woman's name after she says it to help you.

At some point say this: "so since I'm new to all this, would you ladies mind if I sit near you in class so I can cheat off your notes."

They will smile and at least one of them will agree. Now that's your buddy. Sit by her. Talk to her. Follow her lead in class. It doesn't matter if she's hot. It doesn't have to be a woman you want to sleep with.

You don't have to ask her out. You don't have to ask anyone out tonight -- how easy is this?!

The point of this exercise is to walk into a room filled with women, and introduce yourself to 3 to 5 of them, immediately and quickly. With no hesitation. And then get to know at least one. Chat with one. Or chat with all 5 for that matter. Sit by them in class and do what they do (or try).

When the class is over, they'll probably tell you that you did a great job (even though you probably didn't). And that they hope to see you there again, etc.

Make sure to say thank you and goodbye to all the women you were talking to at some point and the instructor. Really, make an effort to talk with each of the 5 for formal thank yous and goodbyes. Don't just walk out.

Now you're done.

If you liked the class, if you found the women interesting, start going.

This brings us to the second reason you're here. You will see certain recurring themes as you read Make Women Chase You. They are: improving yourself. Learning about new things. Having things to talk about. Telling stories.

This class satisfies that. One class alone gives you a story and a little adventure to talk about. You are also learning about something new and doing something to improve your physical health.

Plus, if you actually start going there regularly, well…. it's a room full of women, so….who knows where things can lead.

Just make sure you're friendly and talkative and introducing yourself to new women EVERY TIME you go there. Don't slink back in the corner and be silent. Get to know every woman in the room in the first 5 classes.

Yes, that's right…you and like the 2 other dudes in there…. know all the women in the room…..

Here's another tip. Remember that women are attracted to guys who are really interested in things. Who are passionate about things. So if you start taking this class, definitely talk to all the woman quickly and immediately.

But also (very important) take the class seriously. Be interested in it. Be interested in getting good at it.

If the instructor ask if there are any questions. Ask one. In front of everyone. Don't be nervous. Don't worry if it's a "dumb question." Just ask anything that comes to mind. I promise half the women in the room will think you're hot as hell for asking something about a yoga position.

Action Step 7: Marathon Day 2 - Hit on 2 Women In a Row To See What Happens

Here's the difference between Marathon Day 2 and Marathon Day 1. This time you're going to focus on making the conversations last longer.

Assume. Defer the answer. Change the subject and keep things going. Look again at the conversations in Chapters 5 and 6 of Make Women Chase You.

Have some things to say about yourself. Randomly tell her. Try to make the conversations last 5 minutes or longer.

Get her laughing. Be confident and playful. Fully assume that she wants to talk to you.

Close for the number.

Action Step 8: Hit on 3 Women In a Row With New Openers To See What Happens

We're not going to call these marathons anymore because you're getting used to it. You may still be nervous doing it. You may still need to psych yourself up. And that's fine.

But if you're building momentum and really keeping up with this, you should be starting to feel a little numb to it all.

You should be starting to feel excited when you wake up in the morning. You should be starting to regain that fascination with life that so many guys lose as adults.

You should also be starting to see that rejection doesn't matter. You have probably been rejected over the last 7 days. Are you dead? Will you ever see those women again? Nope.

So who gives a fuck.

And remember this: There are really only two fears guys have: rejection and not knowing what to say. We are tackling both of those head-on all throughout this course. Fight through it and there will be a sea of women waiting on the other side.

Today we're going to do the same thing as yesterday, but with different openers. Here's two similar (but new) ones to try.

"Excuse me. I saw you standing over here...and I knew that if I didn't come say hi...I would literally be kicking myself for the rest of the day.

"Excuse me. I saw you standing over here...and just had to ask......do you get hit on a lot during the day?"

If the answer is yes to the second one: "Oh. So you have a lot of experience with this. How am I doing right now?"

If the answer is no: "Oh. Well what about right now? Are you getting hit on right now?"

Then just continue with a mix of guesses/assumptions and questions and try to make the conversation go as long as possible. The usual 5 minutes each if possible.

Power through it. You're in *on* mode until you talk to three women. Outcome is irrelevant. Remember to reflect on how good you feel when it's done.

Action Step 9: Hit on 4 Women In a Row With Your Favorite Openers To See What Happens

Repeat Action Step 8 except pick any opener you want. The 4 basic ones we've covered so far are:

"Excuse me. I just wanted to tell you that I think you are absolutely gorgeous."

'Hey, you dropped that."

"Excuse me. I saw you standing over here...and I knew that if I didn't come say hi...I would literally be kicking myself for the rest of the day."

"Excuse me. I saw you standing over here...and just had to ask......do you get hit on a lot during the day?"

You can also use your own if you have one you like better. Remember it's not the line, it's the man. And even more importantly, it's taking action and doing something. Having the best line in the world and doing nothing.....well, that means nothing.

Try to keep the conversations going for 3 - 5 minutes.

Close for the number.

Follow the standard *off* and then *on* mode. Stay in *on* mode until you complete the process.

Say "fuck it" before each approach.

Get this done marathon style. This shouldn't take all day. 20 minutes max and you're done. Don't drag things out. Just get to it. This is an exercise. The outcome is irrelevant. The only thing that matters is that you do it.

Keep reviewing and reading the Make Women Chase You course material and bonuses. Try to incorporate as much as you can into each approach and keep trying and perfecting new stuff each day.

Action Step 10: Hit on 2 Single Women and 1 Pair To See What Happens

If you've made it this far, they you probably have at least 1 date lined up already. Props man. You're on your way to a life most men only dream about.

Today is going to be another big step. You're going to hit on a pair of girls for the first time.

I'm going to honest with you. Most guys WILL NEVER HIT ON A PAIR OF GIRLS IN THEIR LIFETIME.

EVER.

If you can get through today, then you are literally in the top 5% of guys already. Probably the top 1%.

Now you're not going to hit on both girls. You're going to hit on 1 of the 2 in the pair.

Before you do it, hit on 2 girls who are alone, using the same methods as in Action Step 9. This will put you in the right mode before approaching the pair of girls.

I'm going to give you 2 openers. They are just variations of what we have practiced already. You pick your favorite to try today. Tomorrow we will try the other one.

The openers are:

You go up to the one you're NOT interested in and say: "Excuse me. I just wanted to tell you that I think your friend is absolutely gorgeous. But I'm not sure what to say to her. Can you help me out?"

(remember: total confidence, total assumption, who gives a fuck)

They will both laugh (in a good, flattered way).

The friend could say anything from: "just say hi" to "say this specific thing" to "tell her she's gorgeous then."

Here's the key: DON'T IMMEDIATELY DO WHAT THE FRIEND SAYS.

Say: "Wow. That's really good advice. What's your name?" And hold out your hand to the one you're NOT interested in.

This will confuse them a little, and will show you're a man who isn't just going to do exactly what you were told to do, the second you were told to do it.

Make an assumption about the one you're still talking to (the one you're NOT interested in).

"You're a Cali girl aren't you."

"Why?"

"Because Cali girls usually give good advice like that. I asked a New York girl that same question once. She said to tell her friend that she was a blimp......I didn't think that was such a good idea."

They might laugh at that. They might say whatever. You just keep it going for a few moments until some point shortly thereafter when you say:

"Cool. I'm going to try your advice."

Then you turn to the other one, and say whatever the first girl suggested.

Then take it from there with the second girl using assumptions and questions.

This probably won't play out as perfectly smoothly as I've laid it out here. But here are some key points I want you to remember:

First, approaching two girls is a fucking bold thing to do. Two girls together DO NOT get approached that often (especially by one guy -- a pair of guys, maybe). THEY WILL FIND IT REFRESHING. THEY WILL FIND IT IMPRESSIVE.

THEY WILL THINK YOU HAVE SOME BIG FUCKING BALLS (which you do). And all of that will override any stumbling you may do along the way.

They will be impressed as hell that you even tried that, and even if you ultimately get turned down, it won't be in a harsh way. And even if it is, fuck it. You were just there to see what happened.

Get through this one. I don't care if you have to jump up and down and scream beforehand and smack yourself in the face. Do what it takes to psych yourself up for this. Do it and you will be the happiest person alive when it's over.

I highly recommend that you rehearse this one in advance imagining that there are two girls there. Practice saying what you're gonna say slowly and with confidence. That will help keep stumbling to a minimum when you go and do it.

Alternative

Here's another one you can try with two chicks. For this one, get a scrap of paper and write your phone number on it. Keep that in your hand as you do this approach.

When you're close to the one that you ARE interested in, you say:

'Excuse me, you dropped that." (point at the floor behind her). Same routine as before.

They will both probably turn and look.

Before they have a chance to really even look back at you in confusion, you walk toward the spot you're pointing at saying something like: "Right here...right here."

The paper with your number on it is hidden in the palm of your pointing hand.

You bend down like you're picking up something off the floor, and then straighten up with the piece of paper showing in your hand.

Then you look at the paper inquisitively for one beat and say: "oh....it's my phone number."

They will both laugh. Then you say with complete confidence and assumption: "That was a good one, wasn't it?" Have a huge confident smile.

Most likely they will agree that "yes" that was a good one.

Then you hold out your hand, introduce yourself, and the rest is the same. Assumptions, deferral, questions, get the number.

Again. They will be impressed you approached a pair of girls. So don't worry about anything. Fuck it. You're just there to see what happens.

And when this one is over, reflect on what a confident individual you have become in just 10 days. You won't recognize yourself from a week ago.

Action Step 11: Hit on 2 Single Women and 1 Pair To See What Happens

Do the same thing as Action Step 10, except switch the opener for the two-girl part.

If you did the, "i think your friend is gorgeous," change to "you dropped that" and vice versa.

When this is over, reflect on how far you've come. 11 days ago you couldn't even approach a girl. Now you just approached a pair of girls (for the second time).

How does it feel?

Action Step 12: Hit on 2 Single Women. Then Hit on 1 Single Woman In Front of People.

For the 2 single women (the warm ups), pick whatever line you want and follow whatever kinds of assumption / question follow ups that you like.

You should be starting to find what you're comfortable with. You should also be finding that you are able to improvise a bit now -- which is the ultimate goal here. Lines are just a place to start because we have to start somewhere.

For the 3rd woman, you want to find a chick who is sitting near people. Or it could be a girl working in a store who is standing with her coworkers. You want to find a situation where other random people are within earshot. Maybe they're even chatting. They are going to hear you approach her.

Even now, after all your progress, this might sound intimidating. Here's 4 very important things to remember.

1. You are starting to live in your own world. You are starting to make your own rules for your life. In your world, other peoples debilitating opinions DO NOT matter. As soon as you flip into *on* mode and say "fuck it," it's just you and her. These other people don't exist. You don't see them. You don't notice them. Their opinions don't matter. You will never see them again.

2. The other people, in general, they are going to be IMPRESSED that you approach the girl. Most guys are still stuck in a high school mentality where they think everyone is going to laugh at them. First, who cares. Second, and more importantly, that time of life is over. Yes, everyone laughed at each other in high school. But in the real world, anyone who sees you sack-up and approach a girl in public is going to be impressed as hell.

You know what they'll really be thinking? They'll be feeling bad for themselves, wishing they could do what you're doing.

Depending on how it all plays out, you could have an observer give you a high five, a pat on the back, or a congratulations after it's all said and done.

3. The girl will be impressed. Because she knows other people are watching / listening too. Most guys are too fucking scared to approach in that situation. They will wait till she's alone. Or they will just give up and do nothing.

This is very similar to the props you get from the two-girl approach. Because what you're doing is so bold, it overrides any stumblings you might have along the way.

So, very similar to everything else. Don't look for the "perfect" setup. If you see a cute girl and she's clearly standing/sitting with other people nearby, she's the one. Go for it.

Use any opening you want. If you're not sure, use the "I think you're gorgeous" opening. Flatter the shit out of her in front of her friends or other people.

The rest is the same.

Action Step 13: Speed Drill. 6 Women in 30 Minutes

Go to a public venue. You can use whatever lines you want to open. You're going to keep it short and sweet, so your out is:

"Hey I have to meet a buddy of mine in a few minutes. But let me get your number so I can take you out sometime." Hold out your phone. Be confident. Assume she will give you the number.

Once you're in *on* mode, you're on. "Fuck it."

You don't have time to dilly dally. As soon as you're finished with one, keep walking away from her, the next girl you see, approach. No waiting.

Right before you flip to *on* mode to approach the first one, hit the timer on your watch or phone. 30 minutes. Get it done.

Again: Don't worry about if it's "the right girl." If you're even mildly attracted to her, approach.

Again: Don't worry about if: *one of the girls I was just hitting on sees me hitting on another girl.* Who cares. You're not marrying these people. You're just trying to hit the 15 day mark. Then we move to night game. You're almost there.

Action Step 14: Speed Drill. 3 Pairs of Women in 30 Minutes

This is exactly the same as Action Step 13 except you are approaching 2 girls and doing the 2 girl openings.

Use either opening or both. Whatever you're comfortable with.

Read this: When you complete this exercise you officially graduate to being a fucking stud. Even if you get rejected 3 times in a row. You will be the envy of all your male friends not too far down the road.

Action Step 15: Up to 6 Girls. Let's do something right now.

It's the 15th day mark. If you made it this far, you are literally in the top 1% of guys. You have more game than most guys will ever have in their life.

Even if you got rejected a bunch along the way. Because rejection is just part of the game. You should be at a point where it is barely (if at all) phasing you right now. This is where we wanted to get.

Once you squash approach anxiety, everything else about attracting women is simple.

This is daygame graduation day! You made it. And I bet you feel fucking amazing!!

So the exercise today is to get a girl to go on a date with you <u>right now</u>. It doesn't matter if you are successful at it or not. Girls are busy running errands and shit during the day, so you may not be successful. That's fine.

The point of this day is not speed, but your conversation. You really want to work on dropping assumptions and questions and keeping the conversation going for as long as possible.

You want to find out what she's up to, and then figure out a way to get her to do something with you right now.

So let's say she's shopping. You can turn it into: "Let's go have some fun right now. I got an idea. You be my new girlfriend for 15 minutes. We'll go try on some clothes. I can tell you how sexy you are. You can tell me how sexy I am. And then we can fight about dumb stuff and break up with each other. It will be fun, what do you say?"

If she finds you interesting and she is really out shopping, she might just take you up on it. Afterwards, take her out for some drinks. Make it into a real date.

Let's say she's just killing time. She could say a million different things about what she's doing, but the underlying theme is that basically she's in no rush. She's killing time. In this case,

"Let's go have some fun right now. I got an idea. You be my new girlfriend for 15 minutes. Let's go grab a coffee. We can talk about how great our relationship is. Then we can fight about dumb stuff. And then we can break up. It will be fun, what do you say?"

You could also substitute coffee for beer in the above scenario if you think appropriate.

Whatever it is, talk to her long enough that she gets comfortable (like 5 minutes) and then try to transition into doing something right now.

See where it goes.

Do this with up to 6 women. If you have success on number 2, then go enjoy the day with number 2 and you're done. If you attempt 6 times and it doesn't work, you're done.

At this point you should have approach anxiety basically squashed. If you still want more practice before going to night game, go back and redo whichever Action Step you found the hardest.

If you skipped one along the way (shame, shame).......now's the time my friend.

Get it done.

Next steps:

You have built up a lot of momentum here. Momentum is very important to success at anything. But you're still only two weeks in. So don't let the momentum stop. Here's what you should be doing.

1. If you are a bar/club guy and you want to master night game. Go to the Nighttime Unleashed and complete the 10 action steps.

2. If you just want to stick to day game, then make approaching women a habit. You can do a little everyday, or marathon sessions a couple times a week. Whatever you like best. Ideally you should just make it part of your life.

For example, you don't go out looking for it, but when you see a hot girl, you approach. In order to do this, always be ready (like always look and smell good before leaving the house) and put yourself in *on* mode before you walk out the door. Just be *on*. If something happens, it happens. If not, no problem.

3. Start approaching women in front of your friends. Show them how to do it. They will be impressed as hell. Teach them what you've learned. That finalizes the three steps of mastery: learn, do, teach.

Whatever you do, don't stop. This is just like weightlifting. If you just stop, you lose all your progress. So keep up the momentum.

Congratulations my friend, you have manned the fuck up!!

Supplement Course 2: Nighttime Unleashed

(25 Day Action Plan to Change Your Life - Part 2)

This is Part 2 of the 25 Day Action Plan. Prior to this you should have completed Part 1, Daytime Unleashed. If you haven't don't that yet, it is highly recommended that you do it now. Finishing Part 1 will make everything below much easier.

Let me start by congratulating you on getting to this point. If you completed Part 1, your approach anxiety should be basically squashed by now.

You should also realize how far ahead you are now compared to other guys. The approaches you made in Daytime Unleashed, most guys will never do that.

Seriously.

Now it's time to take things to the next level. Nighttime is not easier or harder than daytime. It's just different. Preselection doesn't really apply during daytime because the women you're approaching likely didn't see you talking to women prior.

You were basically talking to women one by one. Even when you talked to the pairs of women, it was still one pair at a time.

At night preselection is everywhere. The more women you talk to, the more other women will get curious about you. All the women are watching and looking for the most interesting guy.

The best part is that the most interesting guy isn't the "hottest one" or the "buffest one." It's the one talking to all the other girls.

Remember that you don't need to actually pick up women or even get their numbers for preselection to work. You just need to be seen talking to them. This is exactly what Storming the Beach accomplishes. Do everything in these Action Steps with complete confidence and a playful manner. You're just doing it to see what happens. The outcome is irrelevant.

Review Chapters 5 and 6 of Make Women Chase You as you go through these steps. Select lines and techniques to test out. Find the ones you like and make them your own.

Remember that there is no "best line." Every line and technique can work sometimes and none of them work all the time. It's the man. Not the line.

And at this point, if you've completed all the Action Steps in Daytime Unleashed, you are becoming quite *the man*.

Action Step 16: Storm The Beach - Talk To 1 Woman Before Ordering A Drink

In Daytime Unleashed we discussed the concept of *on* and *off* mode. Basically you were in *off* mode until you made your first approach.

In Nighttime Unleashed, *on* mode starts the moment you <u>LEAVE YOUR HOUSE</u>.

It doesn't start the moment you walk into the venue or after your first drink or anything like that. It doesn't start after you've "scoped the place out."

On mode starts when you leave your house regardless of whether you're alone, with friends or in mixed groups. The way you make sure you're in *on* mode is you <u>start talking to *ANYONE* outside of your group, as soon as possible</u>.

It's easy to talk to people in your group. And you should talk to people in your group, obviously. They're your friends after all.

But it's also really easy to get stuck talking to ONLY people in your group. Then you all show up at the bar and just talk to each other. Hours can then go by before anyone in the group starts talking to other people.

From now on, you're going to change that starting right away. Don't announce to your friends that you're going to do it. Just do it, and let them follow your lead. You will find that as you start talking to other people, so will they.

So talk to people on the train. People you pass if you're walking. The cab driver. The UBER driver. People in line at the club. The bouncers. The doorman. Anyone. If there's women around, definitely talk to them.

Hit on a women *on your way* to the night venue (when possible). Try to get her to go with you and the group. Be playful and have fun.

Turn yourself *on* in advance by talking as much as possible, to anyone.

What you're talking about doesn't matter. If you're talking to women in line, just approach it like you would any other situation. Make an assumption, change the subject, tell her/them something random, get a piece of info and move on.

At night, there's another thing to change frequently. Change who you're talking too. Be interested in someone while you're talking to them, but be quick to "lose interest" in them and become interested in someone else.

Change who you're talking to as much as you change the topic. Think social butterfly. This is what social butterflies do. They're all over the place. And with the techniques in Chapter 5 of Make Women Chase You, *you too* can do just that.

You can always turn back to people in your group to change things up.

You can go in and out of the group (not physically per se, but with discussion). Say something to a friend. Say something to the woman next to you in line. Say something to a different friend. Woman in line. Different person in line. Friend. Woman in line. Friend. Etc. Etc.

The key is to just keep talking. Get so used to talking that it almost seems weird to *not* be talking.

Now you're in the right mode to Storm The Beach the moment you walk through the door.

Say "fuck it" to yourself right as you walk through the door.

If you're just kicking back, being quiet, letting everyone else talk, all the way up to walking through the door, it's much, much harder to turn *on*, at that exact moment.

Guys who are practiced at this can turn from *off* to *on* instantly, anytime. But when you're just beginning, turn *on* in advance.

For this Action Step, your goal is to talk to the first girl you see when you walk through the door. You're going to do all the preparation above. And even if you talked to 5 girls in line, doesn't matter. The moment you walk through the door, you talk to the first girl you see. No thinking. No hesitation.

Don't worry if she's the "right girl." Don't worry if she might have a boyfriend elsewhere in the venue. If she's the first girl you see who isn't obviously standing with a guy, she's the "right girl" for this exercise.

Follow the conversation steps laid out in Chapter 5 of Make Women Chase You. Make assumptions, find out something about her. Spend about 1 minute. Excuse yourself and head to the bar.

That's it.

If you get separated from the group when you stop and talk to her, who cares. They will have a seat waiting for you somewhere.

Do whatever you want for the rest of the night. They key to successfully completing this Action Step is just talking to the first girl you see, as soon as you walk through the door.

Action Step 17: Storm The Beach - Talk To 2 Woman Before Ordering A Drink

You're going to do the exact same thing as Action Step 16.

All the prep will be the same. Go into *on* mode before leaving the house. Talk to everyone outside your group. Talk. Talk. Talk.

When you walk through the door, talk to the first woman you see for 1 minute. Then talk to the second woman you see for 1 minute.

Introduce yourself. Make assumptions. Get one piece of information about each girl. Head to the bar. The rest of the night is yours to do whatever.

Again, do not be concerned at all about "what if the first woman sees me talking to the second woman" or vice versa. THAT'S WHAT YOU WANT TO HAPPEN. That's what you're trying to make happen.

Also remember: these do not have to be women you're interested in sexually. They do not have to be the hottest chicks in the bar. They just need to be the first two woman you see who are not obviously standing with dudes.

You're completing an exercise here, nothing more.

If the first thing you see is two women together, just walk up and introduce yourself to both of them. Make assumptions about one of them. Get a piece of intel on her. Excuse yourself.

If you make assumptions about both women and get intel on both, that counts as 2. You're done.

Repeat the words "fuck it" to yourself every time.

Do whatever you want for the rest of the night.

One last thing not to worry about. Don't worry if you're friends think you're acting different. They will be in awe as they watch you talk to women. They will start asking for your secrets and advice.

Action Step 18: Storm The Beach - Talk To 2 Woman Before Ordering A Drink. Immediately Talk to 2 Women Before Finishing Your 1st Drink. Circle Back With At Least 2 of Them Later.

This is the next progression from Action Step 17. However, now the Beach Storming continues until you talk to 4 women. Two before you order a drink. And two right after.

For this Action Step, success means you talked to 4 women for basically 1 minute each, made 4 assumptions and got 1 piece of information from each.

That's 4 minutes of your time, 4 assumptions and 4 pieces of information. I know you are ready to handle this. And remember, it's not any harder than what you did last time.

In fact, it will probably be easier because you're getting used to doing this.
During the rest of the evening, you can do whatever you want. However, to complete this action step, you need to find 2 of the 4 women and talk to them again, for at least a minute each.

This part (or any of this frankly) should not feel like a chore. You should be finding this entire adventure fun and exhilarating. If you're not having fun flirting with women, what are you doing this for?

For the two women you're going to reignite the conversation with, you don't need to get their numbers, take them home, or anything like that. All you're doing is reigniting conversation with someone you met (1) to get used to doing it and (2) to see what happens.

Throughout the night, you should also be experimenting with the other conversation and touching techniques discussed in Make Women Chase You.

Take progressive touching slow. You don't have to do every technique discussed in How To Touch Women on the first night. Do what makes you comfortable, and then progressively push your comfort zone by adding in more touches over the upcoming weeks and months.

Action Step 19: Storm The Beach - Talk to 2 Women Before Ordering A Drink. Talk to 4 More Women Within 30 Minutes of Arriving At the Venue. Time Yourself.

Marathon day. Prep the same way. Talk. Talk. Talk. Set the stopwatch on your phone. Say "fuck it" when you walk through the door.

Your goal is to talk to 6 women within 30 minutes.

Remember that each women is a 1 minute introduction, assumption, get a piece of information, excuse yourself, move on.

If a woman blows you off, just move on. Nothing gets in your way.

When this Action Step is complete, you should be pretty comfortable with Storming the Beach, so we'll move on to more specific techniques to practice in the next Action Steps.

Action Step 20: Tell A Woman "It's Too Bad I'm Not Attracted To You."

You may have been using this line already on previous nights. Regardless, tonight your goal is to specifically use it with a hot woman.

Head to the bar and Storm the Beach. Make sure to talk to at least 6 women in the first half hour, just like in the previous action step.

This should be part of your routine at this point. You should be finding that the more women you talk to right away, the funner the nights are getting, and the easier it is getting to just keep talking to people.

Once you're done storming the beach, go back to a woman you find attractive. Pick up the conversation where you left off. Use the piece of information you got earlier.

Talk to her for anywhere from 5 minutes to 30 minutes. Work on your favorite things from Chapter 5 of Make Women Chase You. Build curiosity. Build attraction. Get her laughing. Get her interested. Change the subject a lot.

Say whatever comes to mind. Tell her something about yourself.

When she's laughing and you feel like the curiosity is there, give her a pull, like: "It's really cool that you're from Denver. I usually have a thing for Denver girls...it's too bad I'm not attracted to you though.

All playful. Pause for a few beats with a smirk. Look slightly away from her for a few beats like you're waiting for a reaction. Be *too-confident* in your mannerisms.

Give a few beats and then pull her in for a: *I'm just messing with you hug*. Then nudge her away.

Do it just to see what happens.

Action Step 21: Tell A Woman "That's Awesome. I'm Making You My Girlfriend for the Next 5 Minutes.

Same scenario as Action Step 20. Lay all the groundwork. Storm The Beach. Find a woman you like and practice Chapter 5 - Curiosity techniques. Push and pull. Practice your touching techniques.

When the time's right, drop the line: "That's awesome. I'm making you my girlfriend for the next 5 minutes. Put your arm around her and give her a squeeze (this is directly from the touching techniques bonus guide).

(When is the timing right? After you're seeing the signs of curiosity discussed in Make Women Chase You -- think late in Phase 2, early Phase 3. Also, after she says something to which you can reply "that's awesome." Also, you can reply "that's awesome" to almost anything, so this shouldn't be too hard.)

Then tell her that you two should do first date stuff. Like people on a first date always tell each other their darkest childhood secret. Or always establish a secret handshake.

After a bit, make sure to playfully break up with her (push her away). Like get playfully mad at her for something she says and say "that's it, we can't be drinking buddies anymore." Then change the subject to something else and move on.

Action Step 22: Tell A Woman "You're Such A Nice Girl. We Need To Find You a "Nice" Boyfriend." Then Play the "Find Her A Boyfriend Game."

The first 30 minutes of your time in the bar is the same. Storm the Beach, etc.

Once you're deep in Phase 2, early Phase 3 with a woman, drop the line above, take her hand, and then start walking around the venue. Start pointing guys out to her. Joke about how you think the two of *them* would make a really cute couple.

Generally pick out fugly dudes or guys she clearly wouldn't find attractive. Pretend to know things about these guys.

"Oh that guy is totally into fishing. You would be great as baiting his hook. You'd become like a master baiter (don't laugh when you say that….let her laugh...never laugh at your own jokes).

"That guy is a total video game nerd. You two could totally nerd out on some Halo 4. Or maybe even Super Mario Brothers…..that's probably more your style (poke her in the ribs or bump her)."
Keep acting like you're trying to pull her over to these guys. Let her pull you back to stop you.

You can even take it as far as to actually pull her up to a guy and try to introduce her.

Pick the fugliest dude around. Pull her over there and be like:

"Hey bro...this is kind of random, but this girl is like totally into you. She's just too shy to come over here to say something."

She might start blushing. She might keep trying to pull you away. She might start apologizing to Fugly about the "mistake" which *you* just made.

You can keep dragging it out (almost play arguing with her when she denies wanting this guy). Like: "What are you talking about? That's not what you were saying over there." Give a couple teases and then let it go.

"Sorry bro, I guess I was wrong. Peace." Then let her pull you away.

Her attraction for you will be through the roof at this point.

Now change the subject and get into some Phase 3 emotional connection building.

Action Step 23: Play the Palm Reading Game.

There are descriptions of how to do the palm reading game in the Make Women Chase You course.

Start off everything the same for the night.

Get to the beginning of Phase 3 and drop the "you know I'm actually a world class palm reader" line.

Try to get her laughing hysterically with your "reading." Say ridiculous shit.

This game does not need to become your go-to line if you don't like it. Just practice it a bit so it's a tool in your arsenal you can bust out if needed.

Action Step 24: Flirt With A Pair of Girls. Set Up Dates With Both Of Them.

This is a classic that will prove to yourself that you are a changed man. After you do your normal routine, Storming the Beach, talking to lots of girls, etc. Find a pair of girls (who are both cute) to flirt with.

Talk to both. Drop assumptions on both. Change the subject and do all the stuff which should now be very natural. Basically hang out with both of them the way you normally would with one girl you're escalating on. Tell stories, let them tell you stories.

Ask them about how they know each other. Learn about them. Build a connection with both of them. Make sure not to give one more attention than the other.

When the attraction seems high, when emotional connections have been established, when you feel like the three of you are in your own little bubble, close for the number like this:

"You know it's been really fun talking with you two. Let me get your number so I can take you out sometime." When you say "you" just kind of glance back and forth between them, or don't look at any particular one (look between them).

Then pull out your phone and set it on the table between them. Then just wait (too-confident smirk on your face). You can look off in the distance between them.

They will be confused. Because if you've done this all correctly, you really haven't indicated which one you're interested in.

They will probably even ask "who are you talking to" or "which one of us are you talking to" or something like that.

Here's 2 closes to try. Pick the one you like, and try the other one another time.

First one:

When they ask "who are you talking to?", just say: "you know, I'm not sure, you've both been a lot of fun."

Then pause again. Take your time. Be alpha, non-needy, and non-eager (just like you should always be).
Act like your thinking about which one you like better. Relish in the uncertain pause. Let the cliffhanger and uncertainty hang there. Keep looking at them slowly, back and forth, like you're really trying to figure it out.

There's a couple possibilities here. Either they will make a suggestion as to which one you should go out with. Or, they might just both sit there in silence (looking nervously at each other).

If they make a suggestion, you should just go with that. They probably talked about it already (like when they went to the restroom together). I.e. talked about which one is more into you. One may really into you and the other may be just luke warm. So if they suggest which one, go with it.

On the other hand, if they just sit there in silence. Or they look at each other confused, like they can't figure it out. Or they don't know what to say. Give a little time for the tension to rise and then say:

"You know, I can't decide. Let's all three of us go on a date."

They will surely be surprised by that response. It's unlikely anyone has ever asked them out like that before.

Don't say anything else. Be patient. Let it sit there.

If they are sitting there, silent, looking like they're thinking about it. Guess what? They are actually considering that.

They might even try to clarify like: "You mean both of us? At the same time?"

At that point just be cool and confident as fuck. Don't say too much too fast. Assume they both want you and act like it.

"Yeah. Let's try it. Why not?" Keep closing. Tap your finger on your phone: "put your numbers in there, let's figure it out."

Always be closing.

Second one:

This is similar to the second scenario from above, except you just do it directly.

So when they ask "who are you talking to?", just say: "both of you." Say it in a way, and have a look on your face like you're thinking: *they were dumb not to realize you were talking to both of them in the first place.*

They will surely be surprised and appear dumbfounded.

So just continue with: "What, you girls don't go on double dates regularly"

One of them: "Well sometimes, but with two guys. Not two girls and one guy."
You: "Well, first time for everything."

Smile. Be confident as fuck.

You: "Let's give it a try. Why not."

See what happens. Act like you do this all the time. Threesomes are not unheard of my friend. If you found the right pair of women, you never know….

Fallback:

If it doesn't play out that you get both the numbers. Like they seem resistant to the idea. Then just let it go. Don't push too hard. Act like you're indifferent. Change the subject and close later for one of their numbers.

Do it just to see what happens.

Action Step 25: Play The Matchmaker.

This is a great one when you're out with at least 3 or 4 buddies. The more the better.

Do all your usual shit. Storm the Beach. Start talking with as many women as possible.

Later, when you start circling around to all of them, rekindle the conversations, and after a bit start trying to set them up with your buddies.

"Wow, you're really sweet. Let me introduce you to my buddy Greg. This is Greg, he's more outgoing than me. (they make introductions, and shortly after you say) Excuse me (and then just walk off and start talking to another chick)."

Both Greg and the woman will be dumbfounded when you do this. Don't worry about if she's disappointed or anything else. If she's attracted to you (which she will be because of this behavior) she will find an exit with Greg and will do everything she can to regain your attention later.

If she happens to like Greg, then you're literally a God which all your friends will be watching with awe.

Keep doing this over and over. Be the God that all your friends and all these newfound women think you are. Relish it.

Don't worry….all women want to sleep with the matchmaker.

Welcome to your new life…

You're welcome.

Course Supplement 3:

7 Mental Exercises To Get You Laid

You *always* have something to talk about. You *always* have something to say. Remember that right now, you say things all the time. You're just not saying things in front of women. Not enough anyway. That's what we're going to fix.

Throughout the Make Women Chase You course, you will see the topic of starting and holding a conversation discussed thoroughly. This supplement is designed to dig deeper into some of the conversation topics to have you fully prepared.

Remember that sparking attraction in women is non-linear. You can, and should, say anything you want at any time and keep switching the topic. It's fun and challenging. Make sure to keep it positive. She will be uber-attracted by your ability to have a free-flowing conversation.

Here is an long list of topic to prepare you to have endless conversation.

1. Two Stories About You

Telling stories is one of the best ways to communicate with women. This happens in Phase 3 - Fascination when you are building a deeper connection with her. When you tell a great story, people get mesmerized. They get lost in the story.

Women are no exception. She will be fascinated by you when you can tell a fun, exciting story. And it will prompt her to relate and reciprocate stories with you.

You should ultimately have five great stories to tell about yourself. For now, let's start with two.

Take 1 hour and think of 2 stories about yourself. These should be true stories about yourself. They should be funny and/or exciting stories (not sad stories). At least one of them should involve a woman (or multiple women). Think about any suspense that was involved in the story -- like perhaps there was some situation where the outcome was uncertain.

Here's the beauty - life is unpredictable, so the outcome is almost always uncertain. So usually it's more a matter of playing up the suspense, rather than finding suspense.

After you think of the stories, sit down at your computer and type them out fast. No thinking. No formatting. No spell check. Just do a mental dump on the page. Type out everything that comes to mind. Your shooting for ½ a page to 1 page for each story. If it goes longer, that's fine.

Then close your computer.

Those stories will develop in your mind further over the next couple days.

A couple days later, go back and edit one of the stories. Shorten it to it's core, exciting elements. Embellish it with descriptive words about the setting, characters and situation.

Make it exciting.

Make sure to talk (at least a little) about the EMOTIONS that YOU were feeling in the stories. Emotions doesn't mean sad. You want the stories to be fun, funny, exciting, unpredictable, have some tension between characters.

The stories should have some kind of climax (get your head out of the gutter - not that kind of climax). Some kind of build up to an exciting ending.

Remember, you're not writing the next Star Wars saga here. You're writing out a short, exciting, true story about yourself.

Why are we writing this out?

By writing it out, you will clarify the thoughts in your mind. If you can really condense it down to between ½ page and 1 page, you will be able to tell the story clearly, with excitement, animation, pauses and suspense.

Read it through a bunch of times when you're done. Read it outloud. Practice telling it as if a hot woman was sitting there listening.

Practice pausing as you tell the story. Practice being animated with your arms (slow and deliberate alpha movements at certain high or low points in the story). Practice your voice changing pitch and speed. Basically, practice telling an exciting story.

Once you practice it a couple times, you will remember it forever. And don't think that you have to tell it word-for-word every time. You will naturally tweak the story in your mind over time, but the core elements will always be there.

This is a story you will be able to tell hot women for the rest of your life, so put a little effort into this and make it great.

A few days later, do the same thing with the second story.

Now you're armed with two great stories to tell. And the beauty is you can tell them to her anytime (particularly in Phase 3).

The first time you tell it, make sure to notice how she gets quiet and lost in the story.

She'll start giving you those "I'm fascinated" eyes.

Keep the conversation going with your fun, positive and challenging vibe, and pretty soon those eyes will turn from "fascinated" to "fuck me."

2. 15 Minutes Per Day On Something New

Starting right now, you need to spend 15 minutes each day learning something new.

Ideally this should be stuff you're actually are interested in, but have never taken the time to learn about.

If you have no idea where to start, find a magazine rack in a grocery store and buy 3 magazines that you would not normally buy. Start browsing through them for topics that seem interesting, but you know nothing about. Read the articles. Google for more information.

If you're a starving student, just browse the magazines in the store and go Google the topics afterward.

Make a brief bulleted list of the topic you learned about that day and 3 facts about it. Just as important, put down 1 or 2 "emotions" you have about it. What is your opinion? How do you feel? If you're not sure, just formulate an opinion.

This does not need to be an earth shattering opinion. Just something that helps express that you have an actual interest. That you're not just spouting off facts.

Again, you're not writing War and Peace. Just make a quick list. This will help you remember topics, the 3 facts and the handful of emotions about it.

Now you have 2 stories (from Exercise 1) and a list of a bunch of random topics you are "conversationally knowledgeable" about. Remember, actually writing (or typing) out the list will help you solidify in your mind what you know.

You will likely not take a huge, genuine interest in everything on your list. That's fine. You don't need to have a huge, genuine interest in something to have a 2 minute conversation about it.

However, try to take a huge, genuine interest in at least 1 new thing. Learn as much as you can about it.

Be fascinated about it. Women are attracted to men who have genuine interests in things (besides hitting on girls), and who are always improving themselves in some way (in this case you're improving your knowledge -- and you're prepared to tell her all about it.)

Every bullet on your list is a random conversational thread that you can drop anytime. One conversational thread will lead to another.

For example, in Make Women Chase You, you saw an example of telling her randomly about yourself with a line such as:

"I'm Mark Taylor and I'm a sushiholic."

Now you have a whole list of topics you can replace sushiholic with:

"I'm Mark Taylor and I just learned that [insert any of the topics on your list]."

3. Random Questions

You should have 5 go-to random questions in your arsenal. You are becoming a man who changes the subject often and whenever he wants.

As we know, changing the subject not only leaves cliffhangers and drives up curiosity, but it's also a great way to eliminate any awkward silences.

Here are some random questions you can ask anytime (and you don't need any advanced preparation like in the last section).

Remember, you **really** can just ask these whenever, it doesn't have to be a logical time (because with women and attraction, there is no logical time).

Pick any 5 of these. Or even better, make up a couple of your own based on your personal interests. Have 5 memorized and ready to go so you can just blurt them out at any random time.

What's your most favorite memory when you were in 4th grade?
What's your most favorite family vacation memory as a kid?
Who was the nerdiest guy you ever went out with in highschool?
Would you rather drive a lamborghini or fly a plane, and why?
Would you rather go surfing or waterskiing, and why?
What's the dumbest thing your boss has ever done?
What's the craziest thing you did last year?
If you could only pick three places to travel, what would they be?

If you had the choice between seeing the Pyramids or the Great Wall of China, what you pick? And why?

To make up your own, just use the principles you see above:

- Most favorite
- Dumbest
- Pick three
- Choose between this or that
- Nerdiest
- Craziest

Anything that's the "most" like dumbest, nerdiest is perfect. Like, "what is the most ridiculous pick up line you've ever heard?"

Anything that's choose between two things, or name three things works great too.

As always, everything should be asked with your fun, positive and challenging vibe. And you should be genuinely curious in her answer.

Also, remember that all of these questions can lead to interesting answers which can create whole new conversations. Listen to what she says and go with it. Tease her along the way.

You: If you had the choice of seeing the Pyramids or the Great Wall of China which would you pick?

Her: Definitely the Great Wall.
You: Why, you have something against camels?
Her: No it's just that……(and now maybe she goes into some story about the significance of the Great Wall to her)

And I can't reiterate this point enough: It might seem totally illogical for her to be coming to the end of a discussion about the spinach salad and for you to say: So what's your most favorite memory when you were in 4th grade?

<u>Doesn't matter if it seems illogical to you</u>. If she's like "that's random," then you're doing good. Saying "that's random" doesn't mean it's bothering her. It means it's challenging and it's her way of finding a few beats so she can think about how to answer.

If she says "that's random" and then pauses for a response, say: "Now I'm really curious, let's hear what you got."

4. Tell Me More...

You should be realizing that answering "yes/no" questions isn't the greatest way to keep conversation going. This includes questions where the answer may not actually be "yes" or "no" but it's still short. Like: "so when did you meet her?" Her: "last year."

Despite your knowledge of this, you are bound to drop "yes/no" questions along the way. Everybody does it. Nobody is perfect.

"Tell me more" is a great way to almost always be able to keep her talking after answering a yes/no question.

When you say "tell me more" say it like a question with a little inflection in your voice at the end. Say it like you're surprised she didn't elaborate. Say it (like everything) with a little smirk and some playfulness.

For example: "Well it sounds like you're really into dogs."
Her: "Yeah."
You: "Tell me more…(you looking surprised that she didn't elaborate)"
Her: "Like what?"
You: "I don't know. Like what was the name of your first dog? How many dogs do you have now? Do you have a hairless German shepherd who sleeps under your pillow? Whatever I should know about you and the whole dog situation."

Often she will just elaborate after "tell me more." In some cases she may say something similar to "like what?" In that case just spout off a bunch of random shit that can get her talking. As always, try to throw in something illogical. Like a hairless German Shepherd who sleeps under your pillow…

That illogical statement takes the pressure off of her and makes everything playful rather than a bunch of questions for her to monotonously answer. It gives her permission to just talk about whatever comes to mind.

And remember, "tell me more" is just one tool in your arsenal. If you drop a "yes/no" question and she answers like above, you can do other things, like something from Random Questions above. And you can always change the subject (with a question or a statement). Examples:

From Random Question above:

For example: "Well it sounds like you're really into dogs."
Her: "Yeah."
You: "If there could only be three breeds of dogs in the world and you had to choose, which would you pick?"

Change the Subject with a Question:

For example: "Well it sounds like you're really into dogs."
Her: "Yeah."
You: "Hey look at that couple over there. Do they look like "dog people" to you? I'm going to say that's a poodle-guy. What do you think about the girl?"

Change the Subject with a Statement:

For example: "Well it sounds like you're really into dogs."
Her: "Yeah."
You: "That's cool. So the other day I was talking to by buddy Kristina and she was telling me that……"

Keep "tell me more" in the back of your head and try it out with friends or family. Just see what happens and how people react. After testing it out, you'll hone the best way to ask it and you'll get a feeling for timing.

5. "On Another Note…"

You do not need a transitional phrase like this one to change the subject. You can really just change the subject at random.

But keep this one in the back of your mind as well. Sprinkle it in here and there. It would not be good to say "On another note…." constantly before changing the subject. That would make you sound like a parrot.

Keep it around as a fall-back. Like:

Her: "I agree, that movie was really cool."

You: "Yeah I really felt alive when walking out of the theater. I felt like I was the star of the show.... Hey, on another note....."

Then you change the topic to something else.

You can practice that one on friends and family too. Just test it out a few times to get used to it. Then you'll be able to sprinkle it in whenever you need it.

Just to reiterate, you don't need to use a transitional phrase. Most of the time, just change the subject at random.

6. How Do You "Feel" About Things?

Guys don't "feel" any way about things. That's probably what you're saying. And you're right. Guys are generally less emotional about things than women.

So I'm not asking you to think about "how you feel" about things to get in touch with your inner-self. Or to get into some spiritual mumbo jumbo.

I'm just asking you to think about it in the context of stories.

For this one, just plant this seed in your mind. Now as you go about your day and something happens, just ask yourself afterwards, "if I had to describe how I felt about that situation, what words would I use?"

Think of a couple of descriptive words.

If you see an interesting scene. Like you're at a baseball game with some friends. Take a moment to think about how you would describe the scene to a woman. What emotional / descriptive words would you use?

Here's your task. Get a sheet of paper. A sticky note. Anything. Put it by your computer.

Whenever you do this exercise and think of a word. Go to your computer later that day. Go to a thesaurus and look up the word. You will find lots of synonyms. Pick one or two that you would normally *not* use and write them on your list.

Again, these should be descriptive words for feelings or settings. (Settings would be like: ...and the wind was cascading down from over the.......)

Over the next month, get 20 new words written down on your list. Again, these are not the word you thought of (because that's a word you would probably normally use). These are synonyms of that word.

Then start trying places to incorporate those words in your normal life just to practice them.

Why are we doing this?

Great communication is incredibly attractive to women. The better you can communicate, the more you will find women fascinated by you. Being descriptive with your speech just another way to accomplish this.

Also, you're most likely going to have words on your list that most guys don't use. Different is attractive. Being intelligent is attractive. If all the boneheads are telling her the "the wind was blowing" and you're telling her "the wind was cascading" it will pique her interest.

She won't even know why. She may not even pick out the word (like cascading) as being something different. But she will hear it nonetheless. And subconsciously she will know it's different.

7. Body Language

Body language represents more than half of your communication.

A blockhead with amazing alpha body language will pull more women than a smart, rich, good looking dude with shitty, beta body language.

Seriously.

The Make Women Chase You course goes into basic details about different components of body language.

But body language can realistically be a course in and of itself.

So for purposes of these 7 exercises, I want you to pick just one thing to improve.

Just 1 thing can make a world of difference in how you non-verbally communicate with women.

You can pick whatever you want, but I suggest: **Slow Down**

Because slow down applies to almost all areas of body language.

Just slow down. Practice slowing down. In whatever you do, walking, eating, getting up, sitting down, turning your head, talking, moving your eyes. Just take notice of it and slow everything down by 50%.

Now that you're thinking about it, you will start catching yourself doing things too fast.

Did you put that fork down on the table between bites? No? Then you're probably eating too fast.

Did you turn your head really quickly when you heard something? Then you're reacting too fast.

Take note of how fast you're walking. Can you slow it down. Put a little swagger in your step. Walk around like you own the place. Walk into venues like you own the place.

When you get out of that chair, are you popping up like a jack-in-the-box? Or are you standing up slowly, with intention. Like the way the alpha male lion might stand up after 4 hour nap.

You should also start observing people around you (including men). Do you see men scurrying around. Walking too fast. Eyes and hands flailing around with twitchy movements.

Observe them so you can see what *not* to do.

Bonus 1. Physical Exercise

Newsflash: Women are attracted to men who are physically fit and always improving their bodies.

If you're a dude who hits the gym regularly, then this section should be easy.

For you, pick one thing that you've been wanting to improve in your exercise routine, but haven't done anything about.

Pick that one thing that's been nagging at you. The one thing that you've been putting off. Or that one goal that you've been struggling to achieve.

As you go through the Make Women Chase You course, focus hard on that one thing.

Not only will it help you achieve your goal, but it will give you a great story to tell when you're on dates about how you set a goal to achieve this one thing and did it (or are in the process of doing it).

This story does not count as one of the two stories you need to come up with in the first bullet of this guide. This is a bonus story, just for her :-)

I can't stress this enough: Women love to talk about bodies and physical fitness. They are highly attracted to men who are constantly striving to improve their health and physical fitness. So do it. And talk about it with them.

Now if you're a dude who saw some dumbbells once, and that's about it, you need to get started doing something.

If you have some ideas. If you bought some exercise program and haven't popped in the first DVD yet. Then do that program. If you've been thinking about joining the gym, but haven't. Do that.

Just do some kind of physical exercise. It doesn't really matter what. Whatever you do, it will make you feel better, it will make you look better, and it will make a great story to add to your conversation arsenal.

If you're at a complete loss. Just do push ups. The Make Women Chase You course is about 4 weeks long. So do a routine like this:

Week 1: 30 push ups per day
Week 2: 40 push ups per day
Week 3: 50 push ups per day
Week 4: 60 push ups per day

It doesn't matter how you organize the sets/reps. Do 1 set of 30 if you can. Do 6 sets of 5. Do 30 sets of 1 if that's what it takes. Just get off your ass and do something.

You're not going to become a world class bodybuilder doing push ups. But here's the key: You don't need to be a world class bodybuilder to attract women. You just need to be taking steps forward in improving your physical fitness on a daily basis. And (equally important) you need to share your story about physical fitness with her.

Here's my disclaimer: I'm not a professional fitness trainer or a doctor, so make sure to consult a licensed physician before beginning any physical exercise routine.

Bonus 2. New Diet

Don't get too scared. You don't need to become a vegan. Actually, you don't need to change anything about your diet at this point, unless you want to.

What you should do is think of any girl you know. Just a friend is fine. Call her up and ask her if she's on any special kind of diet. Or what kind of diet she might recommend (even if her fat ass isn't on any diet lol).

Then go get a book about that diet. Read up on it a little bit. If you like it, start to implement in your life. If not, just read about it.

Why are you doing this? Two reasons.

First, women love to talk about health and diet. So there you go. Now you have knowledge about a topic that women love to talk about. Another tool in your arsenal.

Pretend you're talking to a girl who totally disagrees with the diet you're reading about. This would actually be great.

As soon as you tell her about it, she will immediately want to tell you all about how that diet is wrong.

Oh and btw she will also want to tell you about what diet you should really be on. Naturally, it's the one she's on. And now she's going to tell you all about it. How wonderful :-) You've piqued her interest and now she's talking away.

She's opening up to you. You are learning about her and her life. And all because you read some book about kale-wrapped bacon strips.

Here's the second reason.

You set up this little scenario so that *a woman* recommended this diet to you. That's preselection. Now your story includes both diet and preselection.

Remember, women are attracted to guys that other women take an interest in. So if a woman recommended this diet to you, the woman you're attracting hears that another woman took an interest in you. Golden.

Another disclaimer: I'm not a certified nutritionist so make sure to consult a licensed physician before beginning any diet routine.

Bonus 3. Social Media

You already know to get as many pictures as you can of you with women. You know to get those posted on social media. Why? Because that's preselection. Women who are interested in you will eventually check you out on social media. And you want them to find those pictures.

Here's the next step. Every picture that you get probably has a story associated with it. You must have been doing something to get that picture. You must have been somewhere.

Whatever you were doing, wherever you were, those are all great stories that involve preselection.

Now you might be asking, "Well yeah….but those were women I was dating or hitting on. They weren't my buddies. I can't tell a woman I'm currently hitting on about a girl I was dating in the past can I?"

Yes. You can. You dating other women means you must be in demand. Preselected. So you can feel perfectly confident about saying that.

However, if you're still uncomfortable, here's your new thought process: every women you're not dating *right now*, is your buddy.

So even if you were hitting on her, and nothing ultimately came of it (other than the picture of you and her), that's still you're buddy.

"Hey have you ever been down to the Red Elvis? You should totally check it out. I was down there with my buddy Tara a few weeks back and….."

[In the above case Tara could have been a woman you were dating at the time or a woman you were picking up. Either way, she's now your buddy.]

Also, when you're telling stories like this, don't hesitate to pull up FB on your phone and show her the pictures. This way, she will not only hear about you and another woman doing something, she will see the pictures of it.

Bonus 4. Palm Reading

Yes, you read that correctly. This is one of the best games to play with a chick you just met (and no guy does it).

Wait until you feel some curiosity from her first. She should be interested in you before you do this. She should be laughing and smiling with you already. You also want to do this with her alone. This is not something for when you're in a group with other people. Think of this as something a little more intimate.

To prep for this, here's what you need to know about palm reading: Nothing.

However, before you try this routine, just go on YouTube and watch a couple videos.

All you're looking for is the general vibe and setting of how this is done.

When you do it, you find some random time to say:

"You know, we're really getting to know each other n'all. But before I feel comfortable getting too close to you...I need to read your palms. I'm a professional palm reader by the way (you're saying all of this jokingly, obviously).

She will totally be into it. They always are. Or she'll pretend not to be interested, but secretly will be interested nonetheless.

In case you haven't noticed, you are now holding her hands in your hands.

That's right folks, touching. Not for just a quick *high-five* moment either.

She literally gives you full physical access to her hands for as long as you keep up the routine.

Then you proceed to give her a ridiculous "reading."

You trace your index finger down some line on the palm of her hand:

"Ooww....um...this doesn't look good." (all playful, little smirk).

"Yeah….this line says…..um…..no, I shouldn't tell you."

Her: "(laughing) c'mon, what is it."

"Well...this line says you were born with a tail. Do you have a tail?"

"Yeah this line says that you're prone to eating excessive amounts of prunes. (half whispering) That's kind of nasty."

So she's laughing. You're joking around. You're holding her hands in yours.

Golden.

Bonus 5. "Have You Ever Heard Of…."

This is another transition for changing the subject. This has a similar effect to "Hey, on another note." Again, not required in order to change the subject. Just another tool to sprinkle in. Practice it with friends and family.

This is a great place to insert one of the new random facts you've put on your bulleted list.

"Hey have you ever heard of [insert something new you just learned about]?"

Bonus 6. Start Noticing Things In Your Surroundings

In Make Women Chase You, we've discussed commenting on things in your environment as topics of discussion. Just comment on anything around you and ask her about it.

It can be anything. A picture. A strange statue or decoration. Someone else in the venue. If you see something and it piques your interest, just say whatever is on your mind.

To practice this, take a moment once a day for the next month and just stop and ask yourself: "if I was talking to a girl right now, right here, what is something in the surroundings that I would comment on."

Then look around and find something. Then come up with one statement or question. You don't have to write anything down or even remember it later.

Every situation will be unique so all you practicing is noticing something and commenting on it.

You might think this is easy and no practice is required. And you may be right. If you try this exercise and find it easy, then you're good. But if you try this exercise and find yourself at a loss for something to say or ask, then take a few minutes to think about it.

Like anything you practice, it will become easy. Maybe 5 or 10 times and you will start finding it simple to identify something and make a comment about it. Practicing it will also make it natural.

Bonus 7. Passion

Practice saying things with passion in your everyday life. This goes back to not filtering. Have an opinion on things and speak about them with passion.

Too many people say things that are statements, but they almost sound like questions. That's because they're stated with timidity and uncertainty.

Practice in everyday conversation saying things boldly and loudly and clearly. Assume that everyone wants to hear what you have to say. Once you assume that you'll find something amazing….they will actually want to hear what you have to say.

Bonus 8. "Excuse me" vs "I'm sorry"

It's very common for people, when they say
something incorrect, to say "Sorry"...and then
continue with the correct statement." Like:

"Yeah I told him it was 50 bucks and then I...sorry, I
told him it was 60 bucks and then I was like…."

Stop saying *your sorry*. If you are a person who says
that, change to "excuse me" immediately.

They mean the same thing on the surface. But "I'm
sorry" has the subconscious implication that you feel
bad about something you said.

Women don't want guys who are sorry. They want
guys who say what they think. And if you happen to
state something incorrect then: "excuse me...I told
him it was 60 bucks and….."

Bonus 9. Stop Laughing When It's Not Funny

People have the tendency to laugh when things are
not funny. Why? They do it to dispel tension. They
do it to try to ease awkward moments.

Laughing when things are not funny says that you're a nervous person. That you are laughing to dispel tension.

Now that you're aware if it, see if you catch yourself making those fake little laughs when people say stupid shit that really isn't funny.

Stop doing that. If something is funny, laugh your ass off. Give one of those deep belly laughs. Laughter is contagious. If you start rolling with laughter, she will too. But if you laugh at stupid shit, it shows her you're nervous like everyone else.

Also, never laugh at your own jokes. Say funny shit with a straight face and let her laugh.

Bonus 10. Find Your Nickname

Identify what your childhood nickname was and come up with a funny story about it. Something hysterical. Practice telling that story with drama, pauses and humor. Nicknames are a great topic of conversation to break the ice, so have a great story about yours that you're ready to share.

If you didn't have a childhood nickname, give yourself a nickname starting today, and make up a funny story about it.

Bonus 11. Your Go To Date Story

You need to come up with a story of an ideal first date. Your Go To date. To write this, imagine you're telling a beautiful women about a really exciting date that you will take her on.

The date should involve multiple locations (such as a boardwalk, restaurant, mall, movie, theme park, ball game, casino, comedy club, bar, or whatever). A fantastic date should involve 3 venues minimum. Ideally 4. Remember that spending time with you in multiple locations creates the illusion of knowing you longer.

The story should be vivid, descriptive, funny, fun and contain just a touch of romance. It should be something that a woman would think: "wow, I would really like to do that."

Write this out. ½ a page to 1 page. Be detailed. Use some of the new descriptive words from your list. Do the usual mental dump, close the computer and come back and edit it a few days later.

Practice telling this story. You are going to tell this specific story to lots of women in the upcoming weeks, months and years.

You only need 1 Go To Date story, so make it fantastic. Also make it realistic, because you're going to take lots of women on this specific date in the upcoming weeks, months and years as well.

Final Thought

As you become the greatest version of yourself. As you start improving all areas of your approach, communication, touching and so on, you're going to start noticing that women reacting to you differently.

This may happen quickly and suddenly. Women are going to start taking an interest. Their gaze will rest on you longer before it pulls away. They're going to look like they want to sleep with you (because if you're doing things right…..they will want to sleep with you).

And not just one chick. Sometimes.

Lots of women. Regularly.

If you're not used to this kind of reaction, it can be quite exciting. It feels great when women are looking at you like they'd like to rip your clothes off.

When this first starts to happen, it's very easy to feel like "you're done." Like "you've got her." But until she's sitting on your lap on your living room couch with her tongue down your throat and her bra on the floor, it's very easy to revert to "old ways" and start following your "old patterns" of interacting with women.

It's very easy to start letting her take the lead. It's very easy to start pulling her too much. To show too much interest, too fast. To start smothering. Doing this can make the attraction dissipate quickly. And once that happens, it's often hard to get it back.

So when you see her starting to respond to you differently, know you're doing things right. And make sure to keep it up. Keep up the playful, fun, positive and challenging vibe all the way to the end. Keep teasing. Keep pulling her in and pushing her away. Keep changing the subject and being unpredictable. Keep your body language slow. Keep your stories fascinating.

The more she starts showing attraction toward you, the more you can keep playfully pushing her away. Keep that up and she will become captivated by you.

Course Supplement 4:

How To Touch Women

Touching is crucial to building attraction with women. When you're interested in a woman, you want to start touching her right away. This Bonus Supplement will show you exactly how to start touching her, and how to progressively increase touching.

First, let's just be clear that women want to be touched by men they find attractive. If you don't touch them, they will actually think that you're not attracted to them, or that you want to be friends. Both bad things.

Second, just like talking to women in a bar gets harder and harder the longer you wait, touching a woman you're interested in gets harder the longer you wait. So the system below is designed to get you touching right away, and continue touching throughout the phases of attraction.

You will see in the system below that touching progresses form "public areas" to "private areas." This means public and private areas of *HER* body. "Public areas" is going to mean parts of her body that anybody (including friends) can touch. These are essentially hands, arms, shoulders and upper back.

Stomach may also be in there under certain circumstances which you'll see below.

"Private areas" starts with her lower back. You will see an easy transition, which you should always use, to slide your hand from her upper back to her lower back. This is you non-verbally indicating that your intention is to move from the public/friend areas to the private/sexual areas.

After the lower back, it progresses to hips, sides of her ass, legs and then ass cheeks.

You will also see that an easy way to initiate a new level of touching is just a "tap" or a "one beat touch." After that, you can touch the same area for two beats. Then three beats. Etc.

You should operate under the assumption that once you've touched her in a certain spot, that you now have permission to touch her there again.

However, you should also operate under the Two Steps Forward / One Step Back mentality. Essentially this means going back to the hands, shoulders, arms and upper back, in between progressing to more private areas. For example, if you touch her lower back, then you would want to touch her hands/shoulders again, before progressing to her hips. After hips, touch her hands/shoulders again, before progressing to the sides of her ass. Always go back a little before going forward.

In addition, touching should be done with an "on/off" approach. Touch. Then don't touch. Touch. Then take your hands away. Touch. Remove. Back and forth. Etc. Etc. Don't just be all over her. Push and pull. Reach and withdraw. Just like everything else.

Also, you don't have to do *every* touch in the system below. Some touches will only be possible in certain positions. You should simply try to progress along the system without jumping too far ahead, completing what's possible and not skipping too many steps at a time. And of course, withdrawing and pulling back.

Lastly, this guide is written based on interpersonal customs in North America. So please be aware of local customs and adjust this guide accordingly in other parts of the world. In addition, this guide is for social settings / dating situations where you're making your sexual intentions known. This is not for the workplace or any workplace social event. Don't touch women at work.

Here's the system.

- Hand shake (with a touch to the back of the hand, shoulder or upper back)
- Fist bumps and high fives (get them going right away)
- Touch the upper back

- Arm around her back squeeze
- Poke her in the ribs
- Upper back / lower back slide (this is where we begin transitioning into more "private areas"
- Both hands on her shoulders / Two arm squeeze (hug)
- "Accidently" bump into her
- Nudging her into things
- Bumping then hugging
- Show me your muscles
- Secret hand shakes and palm reading
- Tuck her hair behind her ear
- Both hands on her hips
- Touch the top of her leg
- Touch the side of her ass
- Touch the ass cheeks
- Show me your muscles - revisited
- Hair
- Where not to touch
- Touches reserved for her - arm punching and elbowing

Hand Shake (with a touch to the back of the hand, shoulder or upper back)

Most interactions in western culture start off with a handshake. The handshake you give most people right now probably involves your right hand. Your left hand is doing nothing.

The first step to improving your handshake with women is to incorporate your left hand. The creates two points of contact instead of one.

The simplest way to do this is to put your left hand over her right hand. So it would be: both of your right hands come together, and then you place your left hand over the top of her right hand. You essentially shake her right hand with both of your hands.

Take your time. Hold onto her hand an extra few beats. There's no prize for rushing through a handshake.

So it would be: "My name is Jack (you hold out your right hand). Who are you?" "Stacey" (she takes your right hand -- as soon as she takes it, you put your left hand over her right hand. Then you hold (shaking lightly) her hand for the entire time you are saying something like): "Good to know you Stacey. I just had to stop and tell you that you look amazing." (You're still holding when she says): "Thank you!" (Then you hold for a few more beats as you begin saying something else. You can release as you start the next statement): "You're welcome (release). I knew I'd kick myself for the rest of the day if I didn't stop and say hi."

You've probably been holding her hand for 5 - 10 seconds at this point. This is more contact than a simple 2 second right-hands-only shake. More contact is better.

The second (and better way) is to touch her shoulder or upper back with your left hand.

Touching her upper back may only be possible if you are shaking hands when she is turned slightly to the side. If you're face to face, the upper back will probably be out of reach. In that case, just touch the shoulder.

You just simply place your left hand on the side of her shoulder (or upper back) for 1 to 2 beats, while you're shaking her right hand.

After 1 to 2 beats, remove your left hand. You can still continue shaking with the right for a few beats longer. You can also put your left hand over her right hand as above.

So it would be: right hands meet, your left hand goes on her shoulder for 1 to 2 beats, and then it goes on the top of her left hand for another few beats.

The shoulders and upper back are "public" areas so it's a perfectly acceptable touch when meeting someone. It's just the way you shake hands (from now on).

Touching the shoulder or upper back immediately gets touching started. The point of this is to just get started. As I said earlier, the longer you wait, the harder it is. So get started with a shoulder or upper back touch right away.

If you're the kind of person who doesn't normally touch people, you can practice this with anyone. Even men.

Like: "Steve, how you doing (your right hands meet, your left hand touches him on the shoulder or upper back for 1 to 2 beats). "It's been (remove your left hand, keep shaking with the right) a long time."

Fist Bumps and High Fives

You should start using fist bumps and high fives right away. Within the first minute of talking to a woman. These two serve essentially the same purpose and you use them interchangeably when:

- She says something cool.
- She says something you agree with.

Here's the secret: everything she says can be interpreted as cool, just so you can throw a fist bump.

Here's some examples:

She's from New Jersey.

You say: "Jersey. Nice!" or "Here's to Jersey" or "I'm feelin' Jersey" or "Jersey girl" or just "Jersey," and you say it in a way that makes it seem like Jersey is really cool.

As you say it, hold out your fist for a bump.

She's vegetarian: You say "Vegetarian. Nice." or "Here's to vegetarians" or "I'm feelin' that" and you say it in a way that makes it seem like vegetarians are really cool.

You can say "I like that" or "I'm feelin' that" or "That's what I'm talking about" to almost anything she says and then hold out your fist for a bump.

A high five works exactly the same way. Just hold up your hand for a high five instead of holding out your fist for a bump.

Why do you want to do this?

Because you want to keep touching, so touching feels natural. You can give her the greatest handshake and shoulder touch in the world, but if you don't touch her again for the next 20 minutes, it's like going back to square one.

So once you've got the momentum going (i.e. the touching started), keep it up.

Touch the Upper Back

You want to touch her upper back as soon as possible. Within the first few minutes.

This is true even if you touched her upper back during the handshake.

Remember that the upper back is a "public area", so you can start touching there right away.

This is really simple if you're walking or standing somewhere. Like let's say you meet her in the lobby of a restaurant. You shake hands, you touch her shoulder. If you're waiting a few minutes to be seated, maybe you've gotten a fist bump in already.

Then the hostess says, "follow me."

You guide your woman to go in front of you, by placing your hand flat on her upper back, and nudging her ever-so-slightly as she begins to walk. Once she takes a step or two, your hand will naturally come off.

This is actually a great opportunity to touch her lower back too. The lower back is the first step of touching her "private areas."

In general, you'd wait to touch her lower back until the "upper back / lower back slide" later. But in the case of guiding her to walk (like to follow a host or to guide her through a door), touching the lower back is perfectly acceptable for a man and women who just met under the context of dating/relationship. So if you can, replace upper back with lower back in this scenario.

If you met her and she's sitting (like on a barstool), then the scenario above doesn't work at the current moment. In this case, you've still gone through the handshake, the shoulder or upper back touch, a fist bump. Now, you just put your hand on her upper back with basically any statement that you make. Hold for a beat, then take it off.

Then do it again. Hold for two beats and take it off. Then three beats. You're doing this to get her used to your hand being there. It also lays the foundation for the "upper back / lower back slide" later. Here's some examples:

"Oh that totally reminds me of something." (pause for dramatic effect, raise the palm of your hand flat against her upper back - make it natural. When you pause, look like you're really thinking about what the "something" is, and what you're going to say next. The hand rising to her back is all just part of the dramatic build up - like it's happening subconsciously). "I was once involved (remove hand) in this group where we......"

That was a 1 to 2 beat touch.

"That's the funniest thing (palm comes up flat against her back) I've ever heard." (pause for a beat or two like you're really pondering whatever she said that was so funny -- like you're looking slightly up and away, off into the distance, in thinking mode. Your hand is just resting on her back. Hold as you start the next sentence and remove): "Wow...that really *is* ridiculous. So anyway, (remove hand) when you were working at the coffee shop what did......."

That was a 2 to 3 beat touch.

Putting your hand flat against her back on pauses or punchlines makes it seem really natural.

When you're doing this, don't count the beats or anything. Make it natural. Make it part of the way you talk and interact.

Putting Your Hand On Her Shoulder or Putting Your Arm Around Her For a Squeeze

As you start mastering the conversation techniques in Make Women Chase You, you will start seeing that almost anything she says can be interpreted two ways.

So let's say she says anything about liking or disliking something

- I think Aerosmith is the greatest band of all time
- Yeah I'm totally into Molly Cyrus
- I'm a huge fan of clean eating
- I volunteer at the shelter twice a week. Dogs are my life
- I can't stand Drake
- I can't stand people who won't even try being vegetarians even once
- I've got a real problem with [whatever]

You can respond to these in lots of ways, but you always have two fallbacks which are complete opposites:

You can fervently agree and be like: "That's it, I'm making you my girlfriend for the next 5 minutes."

You can fervently disagree and be like: "That's it, I can see we're never going to get along."

Remember, you say everything playfully, with a smirk, as a joke.

So how can you touch her in either of these cases?

Let's start with you agree (the girlfriend for 5 minutes thing):

If you're side by side (like standing at the bar), then put one arm around her, grasp her opposite shoulder (so your arm is across her upper back with your hand grabbing her opposite shoulder) and give her a playful squeeze.

The side of her body and the side of your body should be touching when you do the squeeze.

The sides of your bodies will probably be touching as soon as you put your arm around her. But if not, the squeeze should make the sides of your bodies touch. Hold for 2 beats and release.

The movement should start as you're saying the line, like:

"That's it, (your arm starts moving up behind her back), I'm making you (your arm is now on her upper back) my girlfriend (your hand gently grasps her opposite shoulder) for the next (you start the squeeze, the sides of your bodies touch) five minutes (you hold the squeeze for 1 to 2 beats after you finish talking, then release)."

If you're not standing next to her. Let's say you're both at a high top table. She's sitting at 6:00 o'clock and you're standing at 9:00 o'clock. You can be playful and walk around "the corner" of the table to do the squeeze, like:

"That's it, (you pause talking for a beat or two and walk around the corner of the table so that you are now next to her, side by side) I'm making you (you're raising your arm, putting it around her and grabbing her opposite shoulder) my girlfriend for the (your hand gently grasps her opposite shoulder and starts the squeeze) next five minutes (you hold the squeeze for 1 to 2 beats after you finish talking, then release and go back to 9:00 o'clock)."

This is a physical pull and push. You pull her in with the squeeze and then push her away by releasing and moving back to where you were.

Alternative:

If you're at a point in the conversation where you feel some attraction from her, and you want to keep going with this discussion thread, release the squeeze, but keep your arm there a bit longer.

So you're like: "That's it, I'm making you my girlfriend for the next 5 minutes." (while performing the squeeze as described above). Then you release the squeeze but keep your hand there and continue talking with:

"Alright so now we're on our first date. Let's do some first date stuff. (your arm is just lightly resting on her back with your hand cupped on her opposite shoulder as you say all this - just there, not squeezing or doing anything in particular)"

When you're done saying that, then remove your arm.

Remember touching is a progression. You don't want to smother. So while this was a great way to extend the touching while you continued with the whole "new girlfriend on a date" thing, you still need to perform a push, so take your arm away.

Then keep up the girlfriend routine like:

If you want to ask her something to get her talking:
"So what do people do on first dates?"
"So what's your favorite first date activity?"

If you want to move locations:
"New couples should always shoot pool on their first date. C'mon, let's go" (lead her by the hand to the pool table area)
"New couples should always have a first date dance. C'mon let's go" (lead her by the hand to the dance floor)

If you want to touch her more:
"So new couples always need to have a secret handshake" (teach her a handshake - something short, like 5 moves, not something that takes 20 minutes to remember.

Always include a high five or a 'slap-me-five' as one of the moves. Then practice the shake a couple times with her. When the high five or 'slap-me-five' comes, pull your hand away from her like you would with a kid.

If a girl is attracted to you enough, she will do the shake. If she's a cool chick, she will do the shake. If she's not attracted to you enough yet or she's just a pain in the ass, then she might roll her eyes or something at the suggestion of the shake.

In that case, playfully be like "actually, I don't think you're ready for it." or "actually, I don't think you've earned it yet." And then change the subject.

If she flips it on you and says "what do you like to do on a first date" or "what's your favorite first date." You say:

"On first dates new couples always tell each other their most embarrassing childhood experience. You think you can handle that? (if she says yes) Ok, we'll let's hear it, and don't lie.

If she insists you go first, just go first. (But you can playfully resist first so you're not just doing what she says, like: "Wow, yours must be really embarrassing if you won't go first. Did you go swimming in trough of pig leftovers or something." Then look at her all skeptical. Then: "OK I'll go first" -- said as if it was *your* idea).

You both talking about this stuff will drive the conversation to creating an emotional connection, which is exactly where you want to go.

Then, when you do start telling the story, get all playfully-serious and take her hands (or at least one hand) in yours like you've got this really serious thing to tell her. Just take the hand, don't ask, assume everything. Then hold her hand cupped in yours as you start telling the story.

You don't have to hold her hand for the entire story (but you can if it feels natural). At some point in the story you will probably become animated with your arms, so at that natural point, just let the hand go. Again, don't smother. Take the hand, hold it for a bit and then just let it go.

Let's Say You Disagree:

You can fervently disagree and be like: "That's it, I can see we're never going to get along."

Here's the beauty: You can do exactly the same thing as above.

"That's it, (your arm starts moving up behind her back), I can see (your arm is now on her upper back) that we're (your hand gently grasps her opposite shoulder) never going to (you start the squeeze, the sides of your bodies touch) get along (you hold the squeeze for 1 to 2 beats after you finish talking, then release)."

This is nice and confusing. You say something that's a push, but at the same time, you pull her with a physical squeeze.

Remember, you're not really telling her that, in fact, you two would make a shitty couple and not get along. You're just being playful and joking around. That's why incorporating a squeeze works just as well as in the other scenario.

Alternative:

You can also do the opposite. Instead of pulling her with a squeeze, just give her a lite push on the shoulder. Again, you're standing side by side, you just put your hand on her shoulder that's closest to you and give a nudge. A small push away.

So you're like:

"That's it (hand goes on her shoulder, nudge), I can see we're never going to get along." Stand silent for a beat or two. Stand confident with a smirk. Let the push sink in. And then just change the subject.

Alternative:

If she said something really embarrassing or ridiculous or there's an opportunity to be overly dramatic.

Think: a situation where you would put your face in one your hands and shake your head (like: O. M. G. (head is in hand, head is shaking) I......can't.......believe you...... like......)

You can put your other hand on her shoulder while you're doing that. So your face is in one hand, your other hand is just lightly holding her shoulder that is closest to you. It's just resting on her shoulder as you drag out the OMG response.

Even when you take your face out of your hand to continue talking, the hand on her shoulder can just rest there for as many as 5 to 10 more beats as you continue talking.

Then just release at a natural point.

When you do the release, if you are still acting dumbfounded, like you can't believe what she said, just let your arm "fall" off her shoulder to your waist. The way you would just drop a raised arm when you can't believe something.

Doing this will allow your hand to brush down the upper part of her arm as it falls to your side. But since your arm is "falling" lifelessly, the brush doesn't appear to have the intention of you rubbing her upper arm.

Nonetheless, the brush is still there.

Poke Her In The Ribs

This is great for anytime she's being a smartass. Or when she teases you. Just pause for a beat or two after she makes some smartass comment, and then do it.

Here's how you do it.

The first time, just <u>act like</u> you're going to poke her in the ribs, but don't actually do it.

Put your hand out. Stick your index finger out. Point it at her ribs. Even make the motion of poking her in the ribs, but stop short of actually doing it.

Your face should have the "you're being a smartass, I'm going to poke you in the ribs look" - like lips pursed up tight, eyes wide - the same look you would give a kid you were about to poke in the ribs.

Gauge her reaction. If she seems uncomfortable with it, poking in the ribs may not be right for this chick (maybe she had a big brother who poked her in the ribs all the time and she hates that).

If she's non-reactive or laughs or is playful about it (or she tries to poke you in the ribs right after), then this is a fine move to use with her.

From then on, do the poke just like this:

Put your hand out. Stick your index finger out. Point it at her ribs. Make the "poke face." And you should look like you're about to thrust hard. Even actually start the thrust hard. But stop short just before reaching her, and then just "touch her in the ribs."

In other words: you can be overly-dramatic about the whole set up, but keep the actual poke lite and playful.

The point is not to jam her in the ribs and hurt her. Doing that won't get you anywhere. But a lite playful poke when she's being a smartass is a big turn on.

Upper Back / Lower Back Slide

This is a simple "public area" to "private area" progression that you can do relatively early on. You should have touched her on the hands, shoulders and upper back already, several times. At a minimum, you should be well into Phase 2 Curiosity. You want to see some signs of attraction from her (i.e. laughing, smiling, continuing the conversation, turning her body towards you, etc).

This is great when there's a sudden change in the conversational topic. Which should be happening a lot, because your a guy who changes topics a lot. So there's plenty of opportunities.

All you do is put your hand flat against the center of her upper back (just like you've been doing already, several times). Hold it there for 1 or 2 beats, and then slide it down to her lower back. Hold there for 1 or 2 beats. Then remove your hand.

Here's an example:

You're talking about whatever, she says basically anything, and you say:

"That's awesome. Let's get another round."

Now let's incorporate the hand motion:

Her: "He was totally cool about it too. He even gave us two tickets for free admission on our next visit."

You: "That's awesome (as you say that, you raise your hand and place it flat on her upper back, think: center of the back, just below the neck, between the shoulder blades)."

"(Then you turn slightly away from her towards the bar. As you turn, your hand, which has now been on her upper back for a beat or two, slides down her back and stops on her lower back. As this is happening you are saying): "Let's get another round."

(After you finish saying that, your hand remains on her lower back for a beat or two, and then you remove your hand.)

Now let's generalize it.

Anytime you say "that's cool" or "that's awesome" or something similar, you can incorporate putting your hand flat on her upper back. Sometimes you can just take the hand off, sometimes you can slide it to the lower back.

You should practice placing the hand on the upper back until it becomes natural. You can practice it with anybody you know (even if you only know them as an acquaintance).

Just put your hand flat on their upper back for one beat as you say "that's cool." Then take it off. You're just putting it into your muscle memory to place your hand there when you say "that's cool."

Don't practice the slide to the lower back with anyone except women you're interested in sexually.

Remember that upper back is a "public/friends" area and lower back is a "private/sexual partner" area.

That's why it's fine to practice the upper back hand placement with anybody.

Also you should be seeing that by sliding your hand from the "friends area" to the "sexual partner" area, you are non-verbally telling her that your intention is to go from being "friends" to being "sexual partners."

Both hands on her shoulders (shoulder squeezes) / Two arm squeeze (hug)

Remember that everything is two steps forward, one step back. Just because you touched her lower back, doesn't mean that you should start neglecting "public areas."

You should always go back to the shoulders and hands in between your progressive moves forward into "private areas."

She wants to be touched, but not smothered. Make your intentions known, but also give her some room.

Shoulder squeezes generally happen from behind, but in some cases you can do the same squeeze from the front. A shoulder squeeze is the hand placement you would do if you were giving somebody a shoulder/neck massage. Think trapezius muscles between the neck and shoulders.

Hugs primarily involve the upper body, but can have a slight lower body component depending on each person's positioning. Which is good, because some of your transition to "private areas" should start with your body instead of your hands.

Both the shoulder squeeze and hugs move you progressively forward because even though they are still "public area" touching, they make her a little more "vulnerable."

For example, putting both your hands on her trapezius muscles from behind isn't that far from putting both your hands on her neck, which is obviously a more vulnerable area.

So if you put your hands on her trapezius muscles it shows her that she can trust you to touch her in ways that make her vulnerable.

Hugs are similar. If you put your arms completely around her, not as friends, but as a potential sexual partner, it's more vulnerable. She's "surrounded" or "trapped" by you while in the hug.

These are both great after teasing. You say something teasing, then when she looks steamed, you grab both shoulders, or pull her in for a hug, then nudge her away.

The feeling of the shoulder grab or hug is like: awww....I'm just kidding with you.......don't start to pouting lil girl. (then release the grab or hug).

"Accidently" Bump Into Her

This is a fantastic way to advance attraction. Don't quote me on this physics analogy, but from a layman's perspective, I think "attraction" means things bumping into each other.

You can do this almost anywhere. If you're walking or moving around, it's super simple (In a bar this could be moving location, shooting pool, darts, dancing, basically anything other than sitting. Out in the world this is anytime you're doing any kind of walking or moving around).

Just bump into her. There is no particular set up. You can walk right into her. You can turn in a way that causes a bump. You can "get in her way" so that she bumps into you.

You can bump her right in the middle of her saying something.

If a chick is even mildly attracted to you, bumping always makes her laugh and spikes the attraction up.

The best thing to do after you bump her, is <u>blame her for bumping into you</u>. As always, say everything playfully, with a smirk, as a joke.

"Stop bumping into me."
"Why do you keep bumping into me?"
"Quit it."

If you can make this an ongoing joke all night, she'll be all over you. Just keep bumping into her regularly (not so much that it becomes annoying - just sprinkle it in) and then blaming her for bumping into you.

She'll laugh and hopefully start punching you in the arm. If she's punching you in the arm or giving you a lite elbow to the chest, you're doing things right.

Where to bump:

You can bump her with any part of your body. You can bump her on almost any part of her body. The only thing you want to avoid is bumping directly from the front. Because you don't want to bump her face.

For example let's say you're going to just "walk into her". If you walk into her directly from the front, her nose and face might bump into your chest. That's uncomfortable. Nobody wants to be bumped in the face.

Other than that you can bump her anywhere. However, you should not bump her directly from behind (like you're thrusting toward her ass) for the first few bumps. The attraction should be a greater before you start that.

So let's summarize and put bumping into 3 buckets:

- Bump her directly in the front - never.
- Bump her directly from the back - perfectly acceptable, just make sure you've been touching and bumping in other ways first.
- Bump her on the sides or from any angle that isn't directly in the front or back - you can do this all the time.

Let's break it down even more just so there's no confusion:

You can bump her with any part of your body, but do it as a progression, just like all touching.

Start by bumping her with your side, hips, chest, stomach.

As the attraction ramps up, you can start bumping her with your crotch. Generally the best place to bump her with your crotch is on her butt.

So these two go hand in hand, so to speak. Don't start the bumping on her butt, and don't start the bumping with your crotch. But you can progress to doing this as the attraction builds.

What if she's sitting?

If you're both sitting, then bumping doesn't really work. However if she's sitting and you're standing (for example she's at a bar stool and you're standing next to her), then just bump her and blame her for bumping you.

As with everything in the Make Women Chase You course, sprinkle everything in. Bumping is just another tool in your arsenal. If you are just bumping her constantly to the point where it becomes annoying, that's obviously not good.

So be progressive. Start with one bump. See what happens. If you haven't bumped her lately, do it. Again, if you can make it an ongoing joke where you bump her and then blame her. That's gold.

If she starts bumping you, extra gold.

Nudging Her "Into" Things

This is one of my favorites. It always gets a laugh and spikes attraction. This works best when you're walking with her. I put "into" in quotes because the goal is not to actually nudge her into something. It's to nudge her "almost into" something.

Here's how it works.

Let's say you're walking down the street next to each other. Coming up on her side is a newspaper stand, or a street sign, or any obstacle (but I would avoid trash cans because that's gross).

When you see the obstacle is maybe 10 feet away, you start very subtly, walking into her. This is subtle. You're just slightly nudging her over as you two keep walking.

Instead of walking straight ahead, you just change your angle into her, ever so slightly.

You're essentially crowding her space so she moves over. But in a subtle way where she doesn't even realize it.

Then you crowd her a little more, and she moves over a little more. It shouldn't take long before she's basically positioned to walk right into the obstacle.

Most of the time she won't notice the obstacle until it's practically in front of her. Once she notices it, she will stop short and there will be 1 or 2 beats while she realizes that you did that on purpose.

Then she'll laugh and hopefully punch you in the shoulder.

Bumping Then Hugging

Instead of just bumping, bump her and then when she smiles and laughs, or looks steamed (doesn't really matter), pull her in for a hug, then nudge her away.

Show Me Your Muscles

This is great for any conversation where a chick is talking about her being in shape. Or her being a gym rat. Or her being into fitness. Anything like that.

If she's making a big deal about her fitness, you just say, skeptically:

"Alright, let's see the guns." Or:

"Well let's see. I'm hearing a lot of talking but I'm not seeing any flexing."

Or you can doubt her first:

"Whatever, I'm not seeing any muscle mass." Or: "Six pack? (then just start play laughing or shaking your head like you don't believe her)."

And then get to the "let's see part."

"Ok, well let's see what you've got. Time to put your money where your mouth is."

In the initial stage of attraction (think Phase 2 - Curiosity) a girl in this situation will generally be willing to show you her arms and sometimes her stomach. (Stomach may vary depending on what she's wearing).

If she flexes an arm, or shows you that washboard stomach. This is your invitation to touch. Don't just sit there like an idiot looking at her. TOUCH. Make a big deal about it. Take your time.

Actually, if you don't touch, she might just stop flexing or put her stomach away. So touch immediately and drag it out for as long as possible.

For arms. Start by pinching the bicep and tricep. Pinch to feel the definition, not to bruise her, obviously. Take your time. Feel all along the bicep and then do the tricep.

Then go to measuring the size of her arm. To do this, wrap your thumb and middle finger around the widest part of her upper arm. See if the tip of your middle finger and the tip of your thumb will connect.

If not, go to two hands, for example both middle fingers touching at the tips and both thumbs touching..

When you're done, check out the muscle in her forearm. Also, check out her shoulder as well if it's exposed (i.e. depending on what she's wearing).

VERY IMPORTANT: You need to be **TALKING** the whole time when your doing this. If you're not talking and your just ogling her goodies, then it's just creepy, awkward and weird.

So, just to recap. If she shows you her muscles, that's an invitation to touch. But only touch if you're going to start talking right away. If you can't handle talking while doing this, then don't touch.

So, how to talk? I like to go into play-doctor mode. Like I'm giving her a physical exam. Which is essentially what you're doing. Here's all kinds of stuff you can say.

"Wow, look at the definition in this bicep."
"How many reps does it take to get a muscle like this."
"There must be a lot of whey protein powder and egg whites stored away in here."

"Oh you don't take whey protein, what kind do you usually drink?" (if you can get her talking while you're giving the "exam" that's great too -- but someone needs to be talking)
"This tricep is enormous. What's the most you've ever pressed."
"Wow these guns are ridiculous."
"This is insane, you must make the other girls at the gym jealous."
"Turn your arm this way. Flex like this. Let me see it like this (while you're moving her arm around)"
"How many inches around is this?"
"How many chin-ups can you do?
"Here, squeeze my hand, let's see how strong those forearm muscles are."

Stick to positive / compliment type discussion here. If you say something like "pssht, there's no muscle there," she'll probably just put her arms away, which isn't what you want.

But you could say something like this right at the end as a push. So go through everything above and then at the end, jokingly: "pssht, there's no muscle there."

Then she'll put her arm away (steamed), and maybe you can pull her in for a "makeup hug" and then change the subject.

For stomach. I like to do the 5-finger-tip-squeeze.

Put all 5 of your fingertips on the top of your head right now. Tips only, the palm of your hand should be off of your head. Now squeeze lightly back and forth. That's the motion I'm talking about.

So if she lifts her blouse to show you that 6 pack. Go into play-doctor mode. Start with the 5-finger-tip-squeeze. You can say basically all the same stuff as above, just substitute abs for bicep and tricep.

You can then pinch each of the 6 abs (8 if she's really hot) individually if she keeps holding her shirt up.

Then go to the obliques (the muscles on each side of her abs). Give those a pinch. Keep talking. Ask her questions about protein, diet, lifting, to get her talking.

Another thing I like to do. If she's standing, turn her to the side, and put one of your hands on the small of her back and one hand on her stomach, and lightly press together. "Wow this core is super strong. I'm impressed. Do you sit on one of those oversized exercise balls at work?"

Now you've touched the small of her back and her stomach (without clothes on).

Golden.

Secret Hand Shakes and Palm Reading

These involve "public areas" but because they are a little goofy, you should wait to use them until after some attraction has been built up.

If you walk up to a woman and right off the bat are like: "let me show you a secret handshake, she'll think you're an idiot."

But if she's already attracted to you (think somewhere between the end of Phase 2 - Curiosity and the beginning of Phase 3 - Fascination (or anywhere in Phase 3)) then she will find stuff like this funny, different and interesting.

These are both great because they involve a lot of touching.

There is a full example of Palm Reading in Make Women Chase You, so make sure to check that out.

For secret handshakes, do this when she's "earned something." She's done something where you're like "ok....I think you earned it."

These two are optional. You don't have to use both or either one. But they are great tools in your arsenal.

Now that you've read about them, you will find opportunities where using one will feel correct.

Tuck her hair behind her ear

When people think about this, they often imagine that tense moment right before you try to kiss a girl.

You see stuff like this in movies. The guy puts his first two fingers up near that lock of hair that just fell into her face.

Then he slowly brushes it toward the back of her head (away from her face) and tucks it nicely behind her ear. She bites her lip all nervous.

There's a tense moment with dramatic music, and then they both lean slowly in for a kiss.

You can definitely do something just like this later on, but let's not limit this move to only this situation.

You can do this move without all the drama and without a kiss.

For example, let's say you bump her and a lock of hair falls into her face.

When you pull her in for the "i'm just messing with you lil girl hug," give the two arm hug, then release one arm, still holding her with the other. Use the released hand to brush the hair back behind her ear. Then release the second arm from around her.

Do it like you're just helping her out. Like you're grooming her because her hair is messed up. Try to do it WITHOUT any feelings of romance or seeming like you want to kiss her. Almost like you were her dad just moving hair out of her face.

If you do it this way, you touch the side of her face, ear and hair (all "private" areas) but you create no romantic tension (which is fine for the first time you're touching these places).

What if you want the romantic tension and/or the kiss?

In that case you can certainly do the movie example above. The point is not to limit this move to only that scenario. If it's too soon for a kiss, just do the non-romantic version.

You still get the touch in which is key.

Both hands on her hips

This can be from behind. For example, you're both standing, she's in front of you. Or she's sitting in a high chair (like a barstool) and you're standing behind her. It can also work if you're both sitting, in certain cases.

Similar to the upper back touch, you can start with a one beat grab of the hips.

For example, you come back from the restroom, she's sitting at the bar, you come up behind her and say "I'm back." (and then just grab both hips for a one beat squeeze, then let go and move next to her at the bar).

Make sure to say something before you do a hip squeeze from behind. If you don't say anything and just grab her, it could be startling, or she might think it's someone else. So at a minimum, start talking before you touch her from behind so she knows you're there.

From then on, you can start touching her hips for longer beats.

Touching both hips right before a tease is also great. You grab both hips, you lean in close, almost whispering in her ear: "Why are you so short?"

Watch out for an elbow to the ribs on that one. If you get one, you're welcome.

Touch the top of her leg

This usually happens when she's sitting. Imagine her sitting at the bar, one silky leg crossed over the other. The conversation is going well. She's been laughing. The attraction is building. You've made some emotional connections with her. You've shared stories.

You want to be in Phase 3 - Fascination before you start touching her legs.

The first touch can be as simple as a "tap."

You say:

"You know what?" (And just tap the top of her thigh with the palm-side of your hand, like you just thought of something really cool.

Your hand should just tap and pull back. Now you've touched the top of her leg, but you did it without forcing the romantic intentions that would come with placing your hand on her leg and leaving it there for any period of time).

The beauty of that is once you touch somewhere, you can touch again.

The next time:

(There's a pause in conversation, you tap your hand onto the top of her leg and leave it there for 1 beat): "How about another drink?" (remove hand).

Try to touch her legs at least 3 times before moving on. With each touch being longer than the last. And remember to mix in "public area" touches or any of the "earlier" touches. So it would be: 1 beat tap to the leg; earlier touch; 2 beat tap to the leg; earlier touch; 3 beat tap to the leg; etc.

It doesn't have to work out perfectly as described above, just remember the concept of two steps forward, one step back. Take your time. Gauge her reaction. If she seems like touching the leg is coming on too fast, just back up. Don't be afraid to go back to public area touching for a bit. Don't smother her.

Touch the Side of Her Ass

This is just a progression from touching her hips. After you've touched her hips a few times, move your hands slightly downward each time. Before long, you will be touching the sides of her ass.

I recommend that she is comfortable with leg touching before progressing here. In addition, she should be touching you at this point (at least a little). If she hasn't touched you at all at this point, I'd stop at legs and keep working from "public area" to legs and back and forth until she starts touching you a little bit.

Keep in mind that "generally" (and I say generally because some women are quite forward with touching) the guy will touch the girl a little more than the girl will touch the guy, at this point in the attraction building. Like she may limit herself to your hands, arms, shoulders and back. She probably won't touch your legs. The guys hands tend to go further than the girls hands, in general. But if she hasn't touched you at all, then you need to slow down and back up before moving to the ass.

Touching Her Ass Cheeks

This is the final touch in a public venue. After this, things need to move to the bedroom or away from other people.

An easy way to do the first touch on the ass is with a lite, playful spank. You could also do the your-crotch-to-her-butt-bump at this point as well.

You should be feeling a lot of attraction from her at this point. You should be in Phase 4 - Captivation. There should be intense, passionate eye contact. You two should have been touching each other a lot already.

Then when she does something sassy, just give her a single lite spank on one cheek. Tap and remove your hand, just like how you started with the legs.

The next time you can spank and leave your hand there for beat without squeezing the cheek.

After that, one beat and a slight squeeze.

After that, the invitation is open for you to periodically grab her ass. Do it subtly so it's just something for you and her to know about. You don't need to show the whole room that you're feeling up on her ass.

If you're at this point in touching, then most likely you will be sleeping with this girl in the near future.

Show Me Your Muscles Revisited

Here's an alternative to the spank if you did anything with the Show Me Your Muscles routine earlier.

If you saw her arm, shoulder and/or stomach muscles earlier, the fitness topic should come up again.

Why will it come back up?

Because you're a guy who changes topics a lot and you're going to make it come back up. That's why.

So now steer the conversation to her butt. Here legs and butt are probably the parts of her body she's most proud of anyway from a fitness perspective.

When you feel like the attraction is deeper. You can say something like:

"So I know your arms are fit and all, but how bout the donk? Got any muscle in there?"

If the attraction is good (like you're deep into Phase 3 or entering Phase 4) she might look at you slyly for a second, and then stick her butt out toward you.

If she does that, it's an invitation to touch. Give a lite spank, followed by two short squeezes. Then release. Just the play-doctor checking out the goods. You don't need to spend nearly the amount of time you spent with her arms and stomach.

Now that you've touched the butt, there will be lots more to come.

Note that sticking out her butt doesn't mean she's going to bend over. It will be slight. But it will be distinct. She will turn and poke it toward you ever so slightly. She will most likely be looking over her shoulder at you. That intentional little poke toward you is all you need to see. Be a man and slap her on the ass.

If she doesn't stick her butt toward you and she plays it off like "wouldn't you like to know?" That's fine. The attraction may not be high enough yet. But you've planted the seed that you touching her ass is on your agenda.

She'll remember that and will act on it later if the attraction builds to that point.

Hair

Generally you should stay away from hair at the beginning (except for that lock of hair behind the ear thing).

There're two reasons. First, some girls don't like people touching their hair. Second, there's fine line between touching her hair like a friend and touching like a man. There's also a fine line between touching like a man, and hurting her. Let's break it down.

If a girl is ok with having her hair touched, what you definitely don't want to do is "pet" it. Petting it would be like stroking it or twirling it. This is something that her girlfriends would do and you don't want to be seen as a friend.

Grabbing her hair like a man means "pulling" her hair. Lots of women love this. It's can be a very sexually arousing move that feels very dominant to her.

The problem is that the line between "sexual pain" and "actually hurting her" can be quite small. It's also hard to know how much a woman likes that (if at all) at the beginning.

So generally stay away from hair.

However, if you feel the attraction is there and you two are touching a lot already, you can test it out like this.

Let's say you're in each other's arms (picture a dance floor with a slower song playing right now) you slide your hand up her back, and up the back of her head, so now your fingers are entwined with hair and your palm is on the back of her skull.

At that moment, make a loose fist. Just enough fist so her hair starts to tug, just a little, between her fingers. See what her reaction is. She will indicate to you quickly whether she likes that kind of stuff, or not.

If she doesn't like it, she will probably just say she doesn't like her hair pulled. So then you just stop. Your mild tug won't have hurt her, and you can just move on.

If she does like it, she will probably give you some kind of non-verbal sexual response. Like her eyes might close. Or they might roll up slightly (like rolling into the back of her head). Her face will have a look of pleasure tinted with pain.

If she's into it, then just be SLIGHTLY more progressive with how tight your fist is in the future. Figure out what she likes.

Just to reiterate, be careful with the grip. Obviously if you make a vice-grip fist, you could really hurt her, and probably piss her off to the point where she would leave.

So go slow. Also, all you're doing is opening and closing your fist, you're not jerking her head anywhere. Even with a lite grip, you can easily jerk her head in a way that hurts, which would be bad, so don't do that.

Where Not to Touch

In general you don't want to touch her face, her boobs or her kitty kat.

Face - with the exception of the brief touch you might make when moving that lock of hair behind her ear, keep your hands off of her face. Nobody likes people touching their face.

Boobs - If you touch her boobs with your body (like hugging), that's' fine. Just don't touch her boobs with your hands.

Kitty Kat - Keep your hands away from the honeypot while you're in public (you can start to violate this rule

AFTER you sleep with the girl for the first time. But for now, hands off.)

Arm Punching and Elbowing

You DON'T arm punch and elbow women. These are reserved for women to do to you. And you should watch for them. The more she is "hitting you," the better. Remember that every time she hits you (because you're being a smart ass or teasing her, usually) she's touching you.

Printed in Great Britain
by Amazon

45005079R00192